Advanced GNVQ
FINANCIAL SERVICES

Advanced GNVQ

FINANCIAL SERVICES

SECOND EDITION

Keith J Vincent DipFS MBA ACIB

PITMAN PUBLISHING

PITMAN PUBLISHING
128 Long Acre, London WC2E 9AN

A Division of Longman Group Limited

First published in 1994
Second edition 1995

© Keith Vincent 1994, 1995

A CIP catalogue record for this book can be obtained from the British Library.

ISBN 0 273 62056 8

Typeset by M Rules
Printed and bound in Great Britain by Clays Ltd, St Ives plc

10 9 8 7 6 5 4 3 2 1

The Publishers' policy is to use paper manufactured from sustainable forests.

Contents

Part 4 ILLUSTRATIVE STUDIES

Part 5 ASSIGNMENTS

Part 6 ADDITIONAL SOURCES OF INFORMATION

Preface

In the 1990s the financial services sector and education have one thing in common – they are undergoing tremendous change. New products, practices and distribution methods are evolving, as customers and employees alike grapple with new terms such as GNVQs, AIM, PINs, FIMBRA and so on.

This book sets out to help students following the latest type of study programme – the Vocational A Level – get to grips with the products and services offered by the UK financial services sector. It is designed to stimulate them through offering a factual grounding combined with a range of tasks and assignments, complemented by a series of real life case studies. These cases cover a number of carefully selected financial services providers and are written by employees who undertake a diverse range of roles within them. The book ends with a key project – the financial services exhibition – which, it is anticipated, will draw together the skills gleaned by a typical class throughout the year. Opportunities abound to involve the local community – bankers, insurers, accountants and business people – to ensure that the course is both practical and relevant. Whether you are a course tutor or a student it is hoped that you will not only follow the course with enthusiasm but will also find it rewarding.

KJV

Acknowledgements

To David Evans, Geoff Lipscombe and Carol Mayall, my thanks for getting this project underway.

To all of the case study authors, my sincere gratitude in providing such valuable contributions. Furthermore, to their employers, my thanks for permission to print the study with the company name and logo.

I am grateful to all of the organisations which provided photographic illustrations. Many of the photographs were provided by Bromley College of Further and Higher Education. Others are acknowledged where they appear.

Many thanks to my family and colleagues, and the team at Pitman, who have worked closely with me throughout this project.

Finally, I am extremely grateful to all my past students of Financial Services who over the last few years have contributed much to my understanding of the subject and of how it should be addressed at this level.

KJV

About the author

Having spent eleven years in banking working for one of the Big Four, before switching to education in 1989, Keith Vincent is now a Banking Course Director at Bromley College of Further and Higher Education, one of the largest providers of banking courses in the country.

He became an Associate of the Chartered Institute of Bankers in 1982, and in 1986 he completed their Financial Studies Diploma course. In 1987 he participated in the American Banking Study Tour, investigating the US banking scene through visiting New York, Washington and Chicago. An MBA programme at Sheffield Business School (now part of Sheffield Hallam University) was completed in 1992.

He is a Local Centre Education Officer for the Chartered Institute of Bankers, and a contributor to various publications including *Banking World* and *Flyer*. His hobbies include travel, skiing and squash. As a private pilot for many years he has a keen interest in aviation.

Part 1

Building a Financial Services Portfolio

In this section we will consider the following issues:

- Financial services – a key industry in the UK
- The Financial Services option
  - BTEC
  - RSA
- How to investigate financial services
- Involving local professionals
- The structure of a typical clearing bank
- Guidelines on building a portfolio

Introduction

The financial services sector is a key element in the jigsaw puzzle that constitutes British Industry and Commerce. It employs a substantial segment of the United Kingdom's working population, but more importantly contributes to the success of every business that enters the marketplace.

As the services and products offered by the financial services industry are so important, its status for inclusion as a key option in an Advanced GNVQ in Business cannot be doubted.

The two awarding bodies – Business and Technology Education Council (BTEC) and Royal Society of Arts (RSA) – have taken a slightly different approach in formulating elements. Whichever you follow, you may wish to familiarise yourself with the alternative programme. By doing so you will undoubtedly broaden your understanding of the financial services sector.

The approach of each awarding body is outlined briefly here, in Figures 1.1 and 1.2. The unit specifications are also reproduced in full to enable you to compare and contrast them. Read both and you can immediately appreciate the key issues:

- the needs that a business may have
- the products and services created to serve such needs
- the significance of the Banking and Insurance sections
- the range of other providers competing for market share.

BTEC

Unit 12 Financial Services (Advanced)

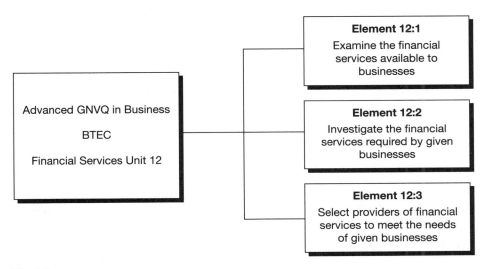

Advanced GNVQ in Business

BTEC

Financial Services Unit 12

Element 12:1
Examine the financial services available to businesses

Element 12:2
Investigate the financial services required by given businesses

Element 12:3
Select providers of financial services to meet the needs of given businesses

Fig 1.1

INTRODUCTION TO UNIT 12

1 The aim of this unit is to familiarise students with the main financial services on offer and who provides them. They will develop the ability to examine a business's requirements for financial services and the analytical skills of comparing different providers from the point of view of the customer.

2 A business needs a wide range of financial services, some of which are required by law and others of which are essential to the successful running of a business. There are numerous financial services on offer from a wide range of providers who operate in a highly competitive market. In addition the specific products on offer and providers are changing on a constant basis.

3 If business people are to select the products and providers which give the most appropriate service to them, they need to have a clear understanding of what the services are, which services they require, who provides them and what the differences are between the competing products.

4 Although the unit has no prerequisites, it will be particularly useful if studied after or whilst completing **Advanced Mandatory Unit 6: Financial Transactions, Costing and Pricing and Advanced Unit 7: Financial Forecasting and Monitoring** and in conjunction with the Advanced Additional Unit: Financial Decision Making. The Additional Unit: Introduction to Insurance develops the work done in this unit on the types of insurance required, by looking in more depth at the insurance business.

Element 12.1: Examine the financial services available to businesses

PERFORMANCE CRITERIA

A student must:

1 describe the **financial services commonly required** by business

2 explain the **purposes** of the financial services

3 describe the **main providers** of the **financial services commonly required** by businesses

4 describe the **terms and conditions** associated with the provision of **financial services commonly required** by businesses

RANGE

Financial services commonly required: finance, insurance, accounting, investments, financial advice

Businesses: small, large; local, international; sole trader, private limited company, public limited company, public (state, local authority)

Purposes: financing, protecting, meeting regulatory, statutory requirements

Main providers: internal (accounts department, internal auditors, company secretary), external (banks, building societies, accountancy firms, credit agencies, investment managers, pension managers, fund managers, government agencies, integrated financial institutions)

Terms and conditions: fees, interest rates, contractual arrangements, security

EVIDENCE INDICATORS

A report of an examination of the financial services available to businesses, which includes:

- a description of the financial services commonly required by businesses

- an explanation of the purposes of the financial services

- a description of the main providers of the financial services commonly required by businesses

A summary describing the terms and conditions associated with the provision of four different financial services, commonly required by businesses, from four different external main providers.

GUIDANCE

Activities for the **Advanced Mandatory Unit 7: Financial Forecasting and Monitoring**, Element 7.1 could provide opportunities for linking with the activities for this Element.

Element 12.2: Investigate the financial services required by given businesses

PERFORMANCE CRITERIA

A student must:

1 explain the **financial services required** by given **businesses**

2 describe **internal support** for financial services requirements in given **businesses**

3 describe **external support** for financial service requirements in given **businesses**

RANGE

Financial services required: finance (working capital, asset acquisition, growth, share issues, capital, borrowing (short term, long term), credit leasing, hire purchase, insurance risk, protection (property, personal, financial), accounting (financial record keeping, internal audits, external audits), investment (pension provision, investment advice)

Businesses: small, large; local, international; sole trader, private limited company, public limited company, public (state, local authorities)

Internal support: accounts department, internal auditors, company secretary

External support: banks, building societies, accountancy firms, credit agencies, investment manager, pension manager, fund manager, government agencies, integrated financial institutions

EVIDENCE INDICATORS

A record of an investigation into the financial services required by four businesses, which includes:

- an explanation of the financial services requirements by each business

- a description of the internal support for financial service requirements in each business

- a description of the external support for financial service requirements in each business

AMPLIFICATION

Given (PC 1, 2, 3) the given businesses are as described in the range, four should be selected to meet evidence needs.

GUIDANCE

Where it is difficult to acquire sufficient information on a sole trader and a private limited company to make properly informed decisions, the teacher or tutor might wish to consider providing case studies for the element. Opportunities exist for linking this element's activities with those for **Advanced Mandatory Unit 7: Financial Forecasting and Monitoring**, Element 7.1.

Element 12.3: Select external providers of financial services to meet the needs of given businesses

PERFORMANCE CRITERIA

A student must:

1 obtain **information** from **external providers** for the **financial services required** by the given businesses

2 **compare** the information obtained from **external providers**

3 select an **external provider** for each of the **financial services required** for each of the given **businesses**

4 justify the **selection** of **external providers** of the **financial services** required for the given businesses

RANGE

Information: product features, charges, customer care

External providers: bankers, building societies, accountancy firms, credit agencies, investment manager, pension manager, fund manager, government agencies, integrated financial institutions

Financial services required: finance (working capital, asset acquisition, growth; share issues, capital borrowing (short term, long term), credit leasing, hire purhcase, insurance, accounting, investments, financial advice

Businesses: small, large; local, international; sole trader, private limited company, public limited company, public (state, local authority)

Compare in terms of: reputation; product features, cost, customer care, benefits

Selection: size, location; reputation; product features, cost, customer care

EVIDENCE INDICATORS

A report on the selection of two external providers of each financial service required by four different given businesses. The report should include:

- information obtained from the external providers for the financial services required by each of the businesses

- a comparison, in terms of all the range items, of information obtained for external providers

- a selection and justification of two external providers for each of the financial services required for each businesses

AMPLIFICATION

Selection (PC4) students are not expected to analyse the providers or the needs of the business organisations in depth. They are expected however,

7

to consider such things as the need of an international organisation to use a provider with branches in the main countries in which they operate, whereas a small, local business may benefit from using a local provider with a good understanding of the particular requirements of businesses in that location.

GUIDANCE

Teachers and tutors should encourage students to use the four business organisations investigated in Element 12.2. Depending on the specific circumstances of the programme it may be useful to work in groups to contact financial institutions to obtain information or it may be necessary for the teacher and tutors to liaise with some institutions directly, with students obtaining the information they need from the teacher.

RSA

Unit 11: Financial Services (Advanced)

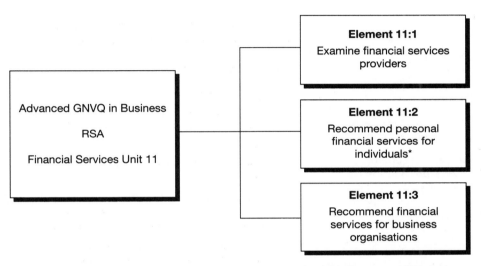

* outside the scope of this text

Fig 1.2

Element 11.1: Examine financial services providers

PERFORMANCE CRITERIA

A student must:

1 describe the **needs** for financial services

2 describe **financial services providers** and the **financial services** they offer

3 **compare financial services** offered by **financial services providers**

4 **assess the impact** of **legal** and **ethical constraints** on **financial services providers**

5 describe the recent **trends** in the development of **financial services providers**

RANGE

1 **Needs:** capital, return on investment, security, efficiency

2 **Financial services:** current accounts, saving facilities, overdrafts, loans, commercial mortgages, credit facilities, insurance, pensions, investments, international facilities (transfer of funds, export support links with foreign financial organisations), currency exchange, factoring, banking facilities

3 **Financial services providers:** banks, building societies, insurance companies, insurance brokers, credit houses, finance houses, factoring agents, independent financial consultants, stockbrokers

4 **Compare in terms of:** value for money, quality of service, range of services

5 **Assess impact** in terms of cost, human resourcing, administration, service to the customer

6 **Legal constraints:** Building Societies Act 1986, Financial Services Act 1986, Trades Descriptions Acts 1968 and 1972

7 **Ethical constraints:** codes of practice, professional associations, regulatory bodies

8 **Trends in terms of:** competition, diversification, impact of technology

EVIDENCE INDICATORS

A description of financial services providers and the financial services they offer.

Notes comparing three services offered by two different financial services providers in terms of value for money, quality of service and range of services offered. The notes should include an assessment of the impact of the legal and ethical constraints on these financial services providers.

A description of recent trends affecting financial services providers covering competition, diversification and impact of technology.

AMPLIFICATION

Credit facilities (PC2, PC3 range) will include credit cards, leasing and hire purchase.

Links with foreign financial organisations (PC2, PC3 range) covers financial organisations based in this country who are able to offer their customers more services abroad. For example, access to cash machines, loans from foreign institutions.

Value for money (PC3 range) covers items such as the rate of interest and amount of commission charged, as well as normal operating charges.

Recent trends (PC5) refers to the last five years.

GUIDANCE

It is likely that the evidence will be based on real providers. It may be that the student will be able to use the knowledge and experience gained through a work placement.

It should be noted that part of the evidence requirements for all three elements could be common across the unit. There are opportunities to collect evidence for all three elements at the same time.

Element 11.3: Recommend financial services for business organisations

PERFORMANCE CRITERIA

A student must:

1 use **information sources** to identify **financial services providers** available to business organisations

2 describe the **features** of **financial services** offered by **financial services providers**

3 identify and give examples of the **financial services** that meet the **business needs** of different **stages of business development**

4 recommend and justify the appropriate **financial services** for different **stages of business development** in given situations

RANGE

1 **Information sources:** financial services organisations, media, library

2 **Financial services:** current accounts, saving facilities, overdrafts, loans, commercial mortgages, credit facilities, insurance, pensions, investments, international facilities (transfer of funds, export support, links with foreign financial organisations), currency exchange, factoring, banking facilities

3 **Financial services providers:** banks, building societies, insurance companies, insurance brokers, credit houses, finance houses, factoring agents, independent financial consultants, stockbrokers

4 **Features:** charges, credit terms, interest rates (fixed, variable), timescale, flexibility

5 **Business needs:** financing (short term, medium term, long term), security, access to funds, support services

6 **Stages of business development:** business start-up, established business, growing business, business decline

EVIDENCE INDICATORS

A report using information sources to describe the features of financial services available to business organisations. The report should identify four examples of financial services that meet the business needs of different stages of business development.

The report should make recommendations, justified by documented evidence, on the appropriate choice of financial services for two different types of business organisations at different stages of business development.

AMPLIFICATION

Short term (PC3 range) is considered to be up to about 2 years.

Medium term (PC3 range) is between 2 and 10 years.

Long term (PC3 range) is over 10 years.

GUIDANCE

The two businesses chosen for the report could be real organisations (possibly from a work placement or visits) or they could be from an outline provided by the tutor.

In order to provide sufficient background material for the report, it is likely that the student would collect material about financial services from a wide variety of sources. In order to prevent duplication of effort, the student could do this at the same time that material is collected for the previous element.

Investigating Financial Services

You may already feel that you have an understanding of the financial services industry, but your objective over the next few months is to generate a portfolio of evidence to confirm that a detailed appreciation exists. If you were following an Advanced GNVQ in Engineering a factory visit would seem appropriate to witness a production process. A leisure or tourism programme would deserve a visit to somewhere such as a theme park. However, financial services is likely to offer a different challenge. You can rarely touch the end product, like a machined component, and you are unlikely to get customer satisfaction in the same way as you would on an adventure ride in a theme park. But hold on! You may already be a financial consumer of some sort. If you have a bank or building society account, then you are already some way towards understanding what a financial service is and how needs are fulfilled.

As you start to investigate the financial services sector, remember that the industry is not only highly competitive, but is also undergoing extensive change. Employees are working under increasing pressure, so your approach must be sensitive and realistic.

Investigative guidelines

Try to follow these guidelines as you undertake your investigations:

- Always explain that you are a student, and that you are following an Advanced GNVQ programme. Indicate which school or college you attend.

- If you wish to contact a local organisation make your approach at a convenient time. Remember, a gap in your timetable, or a lull in your workload, is unlikely to match the situation in the working environment.

- Liaise with your tutor to ascertain whether a group or individual approach is the best way forward. Your tutors may actually want to contact the organisation themselves to facilitate some form of involvement with the company itself.

- If you write to a business or organisation always ensure that the letter is typed and that you clearly reveal your position and needs. Enclose an appropriately stamped, self-addressed envelope if you are requesting a leaflet or publication of some sort. Do not telephone the organisation as a letter is likely to gain a better response. Furthermore, a telephone call can often be considered intrusive by the recipient.

- Learn about the product or service you are investigating from readily available sources before you start contacting a provider or consumer. Your approach, when you make it, will benefit from following such a policy. Remember that libraries, parents, tutors or friends may all be able to guide you if you ask the right questions.

Involving local professionals

As part of your learning programme, aim to forge links with local bankers, insurers, accountants, and other providers or consumers of financial services.

Fig 1.3 Involving local professionals – representatives from a local Enterprise Agency and Chamber of Commerce meeting some students

It may be rewarding to you, the learner, for a local individual to come into the school or college and meet a group or class investigating financial services. This does not have to be on the basis of a formal talk or presentation. A discussion group or role-play exercise could be equally valuable.

As the major UK banks have such a key role in satisfying the needs of the business sector you may, as a group, wish to forge links with the local banking community in an organised way. As a group, identify the number of banks represented in your locality and divide up the students to link students to specific branches. If each student (or a small group of students) writes formally to a different branch, then one particular bank will not be saturated with requests and a more meaningful relationship can evolve.

Write to the chosen branch (remember to follow the investigative guidelines above) and ask them if they are willing to assist you with your studies over the coming months. Provide an outline of the programme you are following so that they can appreciate your needs.

These days the major banks are restructuring and the traditional description of them as banks looks a little dated. The trend is increasingly towards *Bancassurance*. The concept of Bancassurance reflects the emergence of companies which provide not just traditional bank products, but also insurance and assurance ones as well. Consider the chart (Figure 1.4 on page 15), which reveals the structure of a typical high street bank in the 1990s. The type of organisation depicted here is designed to serve a full range of financial services.

 ## *Start investigating*

Look out for companies of this type operating in the marketplace. By understanding them you will develop your own knowledge and be more able to compile a professional portfolio. Retain copies of articles on such companies for your file. They will be useful when you start producing evidence.

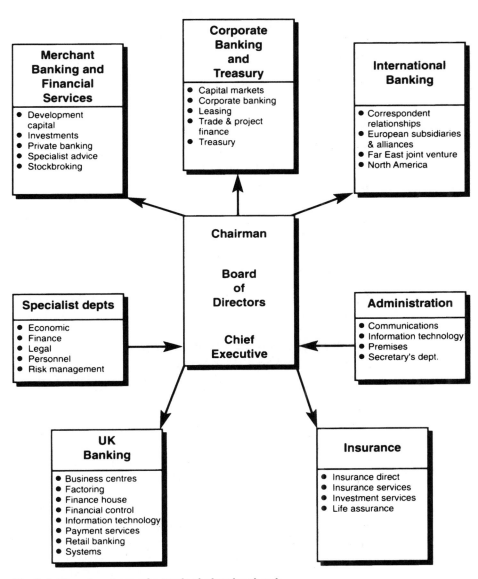

Merchant Banking and Financial Services

- Development capital
- Investments
- Private banking
- Specialist advice
- Stockbroking

Corporate Banking and Treasury

- Capital markets
- Corporate banking
- Leasing
- Trade & project finance
- Treasury

International Banking

- Correspondent relationships
- European subsidiaries & alliances
- Far East joint venture
- North America

Chairman

Board of Directors

Chief Executive

Specialist depts

- Economic
- Finance
- Legal
- Personnel
- Risk management

Administration

- Communications
- Information technology
- Premises
- Secretary's dept.

UK Banking

- Business centres
- Factoring
- Finance house
- Financial control
- Information technology
- Payment services
- Retail banking
- Systems

Insurance

- Insurance direct
- Insurance services
- Investment services
- Life assurance

Fig 1.4 The structure of a typical clearing bank

Building a portfolio of evidence

When you commence this option you may already have considerable experience of portfolio compilation.

Whilst the financial services industry has its own unique characteristics you should aim to utilise a range of techniques.

You may wish to undertake:
- Written assignments
- Oral presentations
- Role-playing activities
- Case study investigations
- Discussion groups.

Evidence emerging from these and other situations can then go towards your portfolio. The performance criteria for each element, in consideration with the range details, will guide you in your evidence compilation.

Part 4 provides three illustrative studies. These may be used as a basis for a variety of learning processes.

Part 5 of this text has ten different assignments; you may wish to use some or all of them. Most are designed for you to follow as individuals, but some offer the chance for some team work.

However, before you undertake many of the assignments you will probably need to build up your basic knowledge. Use Part 2 of this text as a resource, for it covers all the major issues and topics in the Financial Services Unit. When you encounter a 'start investigating' section, aim to complete it to fully understand the subject concerned.

When you read the Case Studies in Part 3 remember that the financial services industry is fiercely competitive. For each company covered here, by someone who is actually involved in providing the service they describe, there are a host of competitors. You will need to identify them and study their services if you are to obtain the wider view of the subject that is required. So aim to develop a feel for the key players in the market both locally and nationally before you conclude an issue and try to claim that performance criteria have been considered satisfactorily.

The Illustrative Studies in Part 4 are designed to assist both discussion in class and individual study. They are based on typical business organisations and show how a business may evolve over the years, and hence have developing needs. Whilst the largest companies in the UK frequently appear in the press, small organisations such as these receive much less coverage and therefore may be more difficult to investigate.

Part 6 provides you with some possible further sources of information but do not consider the content of this section as exhaustive. Look around locally – the publication racks of local newsagents often contain new magazines. The major newspapers frequently contain relevant articles to guide you.

Table 1, linking performance criteria to specific sections of the text, is intended as a basic guide. Once you are familiar with this book, however, it will have served its purpose.

I hope you find financial services an interesting subject and that your investigations are rewarding. Your knowledge, if you allow it to develop, should stand you in good stead when you enter the workplace in years to come.

Table 1   How to use this book

Award body	Element	Performance criteria
BTEC	12:1	1 Describe the financial services commonly required by businesses.
		2 Explain the purposes of the financial services.
		3 Describe the main providers of the financial services commonly required by businesses.
		4 Describe the terms and conditions associated with the provision of financial services commonly required by businesses.
	12:2	1 Explain the financial services required by given businesses.
		2 Describe internal support for financial services requirements in given businesses.
		3 Describe external support for financial service requirements in given businesses.
	12:3	1 Obtain information from external providers for the financial services required by the given businesses.
		2 Compare the information obtained from external providers.
		3 Select an external provider for each of the financial services required for each of the given businesses.
		4 Justify the selection of external providers of the financial services required for the given businesses.
RSA	11:1	1 Describe the needs for financial services.
		2 Describe financial services providers and the financial services they offer.
		3 Compare financial services offered by financial services providers.
		4 Assess the impact of legal and ethical constraints on financial services providers.
		5 Describe the recent trends in the development of financial services providers.
	11:3	1 Use information sources to identify financial services offered by financial services providers available to business organisations.
		2 Describe the features of financial services offered by financial services providers.
		3 Identify and give examples of the financial services that meet the business needs of different stages of business development.
		4 Recommend and justify the appropriate financial services for different stages of business development in given situations.

Parts 2, 3 and 4

In Part 2 the needs of business organisations are considered. As each service is described its relevance to different businesses can be appreciated.

As the range of financial services are analysed so the typical providers are introduced.

Analysis of a number of key providers is offered through the case studies in Part 3. The illustrative studies in Part 4 will give a further insight.

As business needs become better understood the desire on occasions to turn to external services providers will be appreciated. In Part 2 both the internal and external providers are identified at the start of each section. Consideration of the case studies in Part 3 will allow a more reasoned decision to be made as to whether to seek assistance externally to satisfy specific needs. Use should also be made of the illustrative studies in Part 4.

Ongoing investigative tasks set throughout Part 2 are complemented by the case studies to reveal the competitiveness of the financial services sector. The case studies in Part 3 provide a valuable resource to enable comparison to be made with the results of the students' own local investigations. Use should be made of the work done for Element 12.2.

In Part 2, each section considers financial services and types of financial organisations. The numerous investigative elements will help students keep up to date with recent trends. The case studies in Part 3 will further develop students' understanding of current trends and constraints in the financial services sector.

Throughout Part 2, financial services are explored, so that their relevance to meeting the needs of different types of business are appreciated. The illustrative studies in Part 4 will provide a further insight, along with the case studies in Part 3.

Part 2

Investigating Financial Services

This book helps you to investigate the financial services sector by asking you to consider the needs of a business:

- The need to manage surplus funds
- The need to raise additional funds
- The need for specialist advice and assistance
- The need to transfer money
- The need to protect against risks

Please note that these sections of the book are written in a style requiring the reader to put him or herself in the shoes of a business manager. In this way you are asked to investigate business needs of potential relevance to you.

Section A

The need to manage surplus funds

In this section we will consider the following topics:

- **Call accounts**
- **Deposit accounts**
- **Foreign currency management**
- **Investment schemes**
- **Money market deposits**
- **Treasury management**

A business might typically turn to the following for these products and services:

- **Accounts department**
- **Building societies**
- **Clearing banks**
- **Insurance companies**
- **Local authorities**
- **Merchant banks**

From a background of recession the reader may wonder how realistic the circumstance of having surplus funds can be; from a more vigorous economy the surplus may be perceived as a possibility or even a probability. The 'feel good factor' which may well arise from having surplus funds should be enjoyed with caution because all might not be as well as it appears. You will need to know how this situation came about if you are to deal with it most effectively. Ask yourself whether it stems from a normal level of healthy trading or, if there has been a decline in business activity, was this planned and why? Is the holder preparing to launch a new enterprise, to take over a competitor, or is the business attracting a take-over? What other reasons can you visualise? Your examination of a situation will show whether:

1 The excess is growing, declining or stable;

2 The excess is required for a specific purpose, and when;

3 The business is going to fold (perhaps it is a declining industry with an ancient plant which has no future);

4 Seasonal factors apply: pause and consider a variety of practical examples from once-a-year intakes at major sporting venues to the trade association with annual subscriptions.

Or you may be looking at a routinely cash-loaded fund for insurance, pension or other investment business.

Whatever the background your aim is to get the best return available taking into account the time and other factors which apply in your case, and to do so without delay.

Call and deposit accounts

These are often run in tandem with your current account. Commonly the bank has been empowered to make transfers from one to the other automatically, giving you the benefit in your call account of any surplus over and above an agreed current limit, when in credit. Alternatively, you will monitor the balance of your current account, and will arrange transfers between it and the call account with your savings when you feel appropriate.

Your actual return on a deposit account will be at a higher rate if you are able to commit the funds for a set period of notice of 7, 30, 60 or 90 days. Money in a call account is literally available 'on call', i.e. immediately.

 ## *Start investigating*

Different banks and building societies have various accounts available. Complete the following chart for a range of products when you are investigating this topic:

	Bank	Account name and notice period	Current rate of interest (gross)
1	_____	_____	_____
2	_____	_____	_____
3	_____	_____	_____

Foreign currency management

Some of your surplus funds may arise from trading with or investing in a foreign country and in some instances you may face exchange control restrictions or local taxation problems.

You have to decide whether to:

1 Leave the money in the country of origin, on deposit with that country's bank or a UK connection;

2 Otherwise invest in that country;

3 Convert it to sterling and hold it as part of your normal UK funds;

4 Convert it to another currency for other trade use.

The deciding factors will include:

1 The amount of money involved;

2 The restrictions imposed;

3 The likely duration of the surplus situation;

4 Whether local (foreign) use will be the outcome.

Furthermore, you will need to consider whether conversion into a major trading currency would be a worthwhile safeguard (*see International payments in Section D*).

Investment schemes

Here you will consider the types of investment appropriate for your requirements such as:

- Deposit accounts/savings accounts through banks or building societies
- The London money market through a bank or finance house
- Securities/bonds
- Property – your own or other freeholds
- Futures and options
- Shareholdings
- Gilts
- Life and pension covers

Your advisers will narrow the search as soon as your requirements are identified.

Futures and Options are dealt with later in the LIFFE case study (page 115).

Shares as an investment could involve a business in which you have a connection and expertise or may be subject to the guidance of stockbrokers or the financial press, while life and pension covers are a long-term commitment of expenditure.

Most gilts have a fixed rate of yield so their value fluctuates according to the levels of interest rate available in the market at that time. If market rates rise the gilt price will drop to the extent which will yield that return; if market rates fall the gilt price will rise because the fixed rate of the gilt will be that much more advantageous. They are traded on the stock exchange on a cash settlement basis. *(See the section on the stock exchange on page 54.)*

Aside from monetary investment yielding income, there are purely capital gain prospects in property, valuables, fine arts, furniture, silver, etc. Do not overlook the servicing costs of storage, maintenance and insurance in these cases, and the fact that there is often a fashionable tendency which overvalues a subject for a period.

Property has the rare feature that an owner has the ability to alter the investment value substantially by major refurbishment, enlargement or other conversion or, adversely, by neglect.

Money market deposits

Such deposits are appropriate where you have a substantial sum available for investment in the short term, and these may be arranged through your bank. Here again your return will vary according not only to the current market situation, but also to the period for which you can lodge the funds and the length of notice you can provide. The market forces are overseen and controlled by the Bank of England raising and lowering interest rates and thus controlling supply. The market is short term and it is a 'wholesale' operation accessible only through financial businesses.

Start investigating

In Part 1 it was suggested that you form a link with a local bank to provide you with information throughout the year. Contact this bank, either individually or on behalf of a group in your class, and ascertain the following money market rates:

1 £1,000,000 for one month   _____

2   £500,000 for two months _____

3 £1,000,000 for six months _____

Note the date of your investigations . . / . . / . .

Treasury management

One of the key managers in many large companies is the Corporate Treasurer. His or her role will involve the management of the finances of the company (or perhaps a group of companies) on a daily, almost hourly, basis. Surplus funds if substantial, will be invested overnight, or alternatively additional sources of funds will be tapped to cover any shortfall. If the company trades internationally, then exchange risks must also be considered. Exposure to the uncertainty of future money flows and their values, in a range of currencies, may need to be hedged, i.e. protected against.

Treasury management may therefore involve the efficient use of the world's money markets accessed by computers, telex and telephone, to get the best possible return at any given point in time.

Accounts department

We have seen above the role of the Corporate Treasurer or Financial Director employed where the scale of the business justifies the role. In a smaller company the internal accountant or manager will have a vital day-to-day role handling the cash flow, minimising the overdraft, keeping a tight rein on credit control and thus creating or maximising surplus funds for best short- or medium-term benefit. This will include the programming of fixed and fluctuating credit facilities and outgoings, including any currency commitments of the business.

An efficient accounts department is, by definition, cost effective although its benefits are not always apparent because a surplus fund achieved at a certain level for a particular period of time needs to be recognised as an achievement, not as an automatic product. Credit where credit is due still has to be worked for!

Building societies

Building societies are in the market for your surplus funds and you will often expect to deal with most of them for specific round sum packages for a set term (e.g. £10,000 for six months) rather than any fluctuating arrangement.

A few societies do offer more flexible accounts for a business, and allow frequent payments in and out.

Start investigating

Consider four building societies represented in your area and indicate whether they offer accounts for the surplus funds of a business.

	Society name	Product name	Brief details
1	_____	_____	_____
2	_____	_____	_____
3	_____	_____	_____

Clearing banks

For surplus fund purposes the clearing banks (also known as high street banks) will offer terms for deposits. Their rates may show slight variations depending on duration and size of deposit and it may or may not be preferable to look outside your own bank for tactical financial reasons.

Start investigating

In the sections on Money Market Deposits and Call and Deposit Accounts (earlier in this section), you were asked to consider different banks and schemes. When a group of you in your class have done this, complete the section below.

The highest rates for different situations:

	Provider	Interest rate	Scheme	Date of investigation
1	_____	_____	_____	_____
2	_____	_____	_____	_____
3	_____	_____	_____	_____

N.B. You need to know the date as interest rates fluctuate – unless you all did your research at the same time, the comparisons might not be totally realistic.

Foreign banks

These have funds of their customers which they may prefer to invest in the UK. Equally, they may seek funds from the UK for their trading abroad, so you may have attractive terms offered.

Start investigating

Listed below are the names of four foreign banks from different countries. For each bank decide on their country of origin:

	Name	Country
1	MITSUI BANK	_____
2	CITIBANK	_____
3	DRESDNER BANK	_____
4	CREDIT AGRICOLE	_____

Local authorities

A local authority may seek to raise funds by offering an attractive interest rate for a set period of time; if its programme matches your needs there is a real prospect here. These bond schemes tend to arise from time to time and appear in press advertising. They are not always readily available but they do offer excellent security along with a competitive rate and they fix the date for repayment.

Merchant banks

Merchant banks will offer terms and will put your business money to work. It might be a worthwhile exercise for you if at some later time there is a prospect of you:

- needing finance from their sources in the future;
- needing their expertise and backing for a share issue, i.e. an offer of your shares to the public;
- wanting to use their expertise in a take-over.

Originally the merchant bankers were primarily merchants who acquired considerable local knowledge and expertise related to particular overseas markets, and they put this knowledge to commercial use in guiding and lending to other traders. The successful ones prospered more from the application of this expertise than from their own direct trading enterprises.

Their expertise generally is in lending the funds which they have been instructed to manage (especially pension funds) or have otherwise acquired from the money market.

Section B

The need to raise additional funds

In this section we will consider the following topics:

- **Associated companies**
- **Business angels**
- **Business loans**
- **Commercial mortgages**
- **Costs of borrowing**
- **Credit**
- **Debentures**
- **Factoring**
- **Finance houses**
- **Hire purchase**
- **Leasing**
- **Long-term borrowing**
- **Mergers and take-overs**
- **Overdrafts**
- **Security for borrowing**
- **Share issues**
- **Short-term borrowing**
- **Start-up capital**
- **Stock exchanges**
- **Venture capital**
- **Working capital**

A business might typically turn to the following for these products and services:

- **Building societies**
- **Clearing banks**
- **Factors**
- **Finance houses**
- **Foreign banks**
- **Hire purchase companies**
- **Leasing companies**
- **LINC (see Business angels)**
- **Merchant banks**
- **Stock exchanges**
- **Venture capitalists**

You have established that you need to raise additional funds and must decide how much money you require by preparing a business plan and a forecast of the probable programme of monies in and out of your business.

You may be starting up a venture or you may be in an on-going trading situation. You may be in a period of growth and may well find that the profits of the business are sufficient to sustain your present level of activity but would not be sufficient to meet the extra costs of expansion.

The extra costs you could incur if your business were to expand include:

- equipment costs
- premises costs
- personnel costs
- raw material costs
- production costs
- sales costs
- distribution costs
- credit on sales
- financial costs

Additional funds would be required until the benefits of larger scale trading catch up and profitability is high enough to compensate for the increases.

Or you may be in a period of stagnation. There are bills to be met and you are already struggling to make ends meet. If your outlook is not more favourable few financial aids will be open to you and specialist advice for merger prospects might be needed or you may be in a position where closure is unavoidable.

Your assessment will aim to establish how much you require, how long you need it and whether you have the security and prospects that will attract the help of a lender.

If you are a new venture you may find that each of the main clearing banks has a special unit geared to guide you. *(See Start-up Capital and Venture Capital.)* Banks do have special schemes for particular professionals and trades, e.g. farmers and doctors.

If you are established you may be tempted to raise funds by selling a valuable fixed asset – your freehold premises. This is a once only and

Fig 2.1 Do you need to spend more on equipment, raw materials and personnel?

once and for all measure which must not be undertaken lightly for you are setting out to sell and to lease back which commits you henceforth to the constraints of a lease and the need to pay rent.

Nevertheless there are arguments in favour. You may say that your purpose in business is the manufacture of a product, not the maintenance of valuable property as a major asset.

Commercial property has experienced wild fluctuations in value and, as a result, timing will be crucial to feasibility here and the guidance of a commercial property surveyor may be necessary.

There is a worst possible scenario. Entrepreneurial powers may have been abused. There may be a concealed structure of inter-linked businesses, of loans and transactions and other transfers between them, complex issues involving security, even abuse of pension fund monies. This is an extreme, but you are in the real world and would do well to spot the signs and to act to protect your business interests; you may even identify an example of this type of problem.

A common requirement throughout this section will be a *cash flow*. If you are not asked for it you may still find it a useful tool for your own guidance and efficiency so we will examine this first.

Cash flow

This is your forecast of the inward and outward movements of the monies of your business.

Just like a domestic budget or a child's pocket money, there will be the more affluent moments and times of pressure. Your aim will be to manage the movements to your greatest advantage or your least disadvantage. A tool for this, and one which will often be a first requisite of a prospective lender, is a cash flow forecast. This is a forecast of the inward and outward movements of the monies of your business.

In its simplest form it can comprise a year's calendar with each month having:

1 An opening balance (from the previous month)

2 A variety of receipts from:
   - cash sales
   - debtors
   - VAT
   - other

3 Payments to:
   - your suppliers (cash or credit)
   - wages/salaries
   - PAYE and National Insurance
   - other tax
   - rent and rates
   - heat and light

- finance charges
- VAT
- other

1 plus 2 minus 3 gives you your closing balance which is, of course, the opening balance for the next month.

The resulting figure will tell you whether you must defer any payments or must take steps to improve your receipt programme.

What would be the factors you would need to bear in mind when making your judgement?

Remember that you have prepared a forecast, not a rigid programme. There will be changes and some could be totally unexpected. Should you be pessimistic or optimistic in your approach?

The need for a cash flow arises in some of the following sections.

High/low gearing

A company with a considerable borrowing in relation to its share capital is referred to as 'highly geared'. If a highly geared company is not profitable it will be in difficulties in financing its loans: if interest rates are on the increase it will become increasingly vulnerable while a 'low geared' company will be facing a less critical situation.

Current assets

Here it is usual to start off with the most liquid:

- cash in hand,
- then cash at bank,
- stock, and
- debtors

Fixed assets

You will have a formal record of any of the assets which are already pledged or 'charged'. Typically your freehold or leasehold premises will be the first commitment for loan facilities. Is there scope to develop this to a greater extent?

Property

As well as the freehold there is security and investment value in a long lease which is not vulnerable to periodic rent reviews, or is faced with reviews at long intervals (e.g. 21 years). This is because the effects of inflation will have lifted 'rack rentals' (the present value) above the price which the lessee is contracted to pay.

Sub-letting will usually require the permission of the landlord and this may not be given if double or multiple occupancy is considered undesirable or unsafe. Consigning a lease (to another occupier in your place) will also require the landlord's consent, but the law will not allow his consent to be unreasonably withheld. So, in practice, if your present premises are too large and too costly, you may be able to sub-let the space which you do not need or you may be able to find an alternative tenant and would then need alternative accommodation for yourself.

An F R & I (full repairing and insuring obligations are tenant's cost) lease is commonly used but not in any standard form – each lease is ·different in context and therefore requires careful legal consideration.

Plant and equipment

Specific plant and equipment may be committed to the purchase arrangements originally employed *(see Leasing etc.)*.

Debtors and stock

Debtors are usually acceptable whilst stock is less attractive to the banker. This is because a reliable proportion of debtors can be expected to produce cash receipts without special effort or expense whilst stocks of materials have to be sold off.

If there is no clear cut acceptable asset the lender may be satisfied with a 'General Charge' over the business which is secondary to the specific charges and can operate only over the balance of worth over and above that level. (For example, a piece of machinery may have a worth in excess of the outstanding loan which you have on it.)

You may be asked for a personal guarantee as further security. Your aim will be to avoid this commitment if at all possible.

Associated companies

Each company is a separate legal entity and may be independent in its existence.

Often, however, the company is owned by another and may have to trade on its own merits or may have the support of group accounting.

Clearly, where a member of the group has a need for funds which can be linked to a surplus elsewhere in the group there will be both a saving in the cost of the finance and a lack of strict formal commitment which might leave a precious asset free of financial ties and thus capable of supporting other funding. There is also likely to be a less rigid repayment and interest programme.

Similarly, the associate company may be the owner of a substantial unencumbered asset which can be committed to the cause of the group's less advantaged member.

Business angels

Business angels are wealthy individuals who may be persuaded to invest their personal monies in your business. The most commonly publicised angels are those who succeed or fail, with often spectacular and therefore newsworthy results, in London (and other) theatre productions. Most of the investments made by business angels are done more discreetly in all areas of business and commerce.

Business angels may possibly respond to you or your adviser's advertisements in the financial or local press or may, through box number anonymity, seek prospects for themselves.

Fig 2.2 A business angel will carefully consider your proposal

The difficulties are:

- locating them
- gaining their support
- avoiding loss of control of the business to them.

Difficulties in location of the angel by the borrower and vice versa make this a very imperfect market. Some say that word of mouth, chance or cultivated professional encounters at a local level are the best hopes.

LINC (Local Investment Networking Company) is a system run by agencies in various parts of the UK which aims to bring applicants and potential angels together. Once introduced the potential deal is very much a personal matter – the two parties should have a good working relationship and a mutual trust sufficient to cope with adjustments needed along the way.

Start investigating

Consider the best way to present a profile and business plan to a possible angel who may:

1 have an expertise in your type of business (and therefore a prospect of personal as well as financial contribution)

2 have no previous experience comparable with your plans

3 expect concise factual and realistic statements of intent.

Business loans

These no longer flow with ease following an approach to your local bank manager. Reorganised centralised banking controls now usually divert you to a regional head office and a commercial manager.

You will certainly have to prepare your case with care, with a clear certainty that your business has every prospect of 'servicing' (i.e. paying for) the loan out of its profits.

A good performance within all of the agreed limits of payment and repayment combined with a proven track record in business matching or bettering earlier forecasts, is the surest way of success on a subsequent occasion.

It will almost always be found that caution by the prospective lender will appear as an insurmountable problem, but it is worth remembering that:

1 Banks are institutions whose principal activity is lending money.

2 There is a price at which a given level of risk is acceptable.

3 A share of the equity might make all the difference.

4 A Loan Guarantee Scheme, government inspired for small firms, may be an answer where security or a previous track record are unavailable.

In a modest way there is the possible support of the Prince of Wales Youth Business Trust (PYBT) opened in 1983 and this aims to provide grant and modest expansion loan benefits for individuals with a good and potentially viable idea for commerce. The upper age limit is twenty-six, and you may expect a loan to last for three years with no interest charged in the first twelve months.

Often this will involve a chance to offer a service or scale of supply ignored by existing traders rather than an actual new product. These funds will be targeted at equipment rather than provision of working capital.

You should also make enquiries about any help available from Enterprise Agencies, Local Authorities and Regional Development Boards.

Commercial mortgages

These are granted to business borrowers in the same way as building societies and banks operate private house funds. The borrower has to satisfy the lender that the financial position is sufficiently healthy to cover:

1 an initial part payment, and
2 the periodic payments of interest on the loan and of the repayment of the loan itself.

You in business will consider purchase rather than rent if:

1 you can afford the outlay of, say, 20 per cent of cost
2 the freehold is available to you
3 the premises are adequate in size, calibre and location for your future needs
4 you can afford the repayments on a fixed or variable interest basis.

If you own your own freehold this is reflected in the fixed assets of your balance sheet and therefore strengthens your financial status; it may be used for security beyond that committed to your mortgage.

Costs of borrowing

APR is the Annual Percentage Rate quoted in a lender's advertising, and financiers have to calculate it on an established basis incorporating any fees to ensure that it is truly comparable.

Base rate is the rate of interest on which bank loan charges are set. They will usually fix their price as a percentage above base rate. Base rate fluctuates but is usually common to all of the banks so it is possible to compare prices by comparing the margin (their additional interest above base).

LIBOR (London Inter Bank Offered Rate) is an alternative to a base rate contract and it also fluctuates according to market conditions. Although different rates are quoted for differing loan periods, e.g. a three-month LIBOR or a six-month LIBOR, the normal benchmark used is a three-month LIBOR. Such rates are more likely to be used for larger commercial businesses.

These two tools provide a level for ready comparison.

In addition to the interest charges there may be:

1 An introductory or initial fee (arrangement fee).
2 Fees, including legal costs.
3 Penalties for default.
4 Extra charges for varying the amount or period.

Credit

In commerce, credit is the period of time elapsing between delivery of the goods or services and payment of the invoice. It varies from trade to trade and where agreed periods are exceeded the adverse effect on the supplier's cash flow (*see page 42*) is readily apparent. However, if you are under financial pressure, you may find that your supplier is able to agree to extending your credit facilities on a goodwill basis, usually only where a regular business relationship exists. To be able to settle in ninety days instead of monthly is clearly advantageous and you could compile alternative cash flows to illustrate the difference.

In instances of major goods retailing (for example, furniture, cars) the manufacturer may find it advantageous to give extended credit. In practice he will find benefits in trade in having his product stored by you, the retailer, being nearer the ultimate customer, than at his warehouse. He will then usually require that ownership of the items remain his until payment is made.

Formal financial credit can be provided by merchant banks and finance houses through the use of *bills of exchange*. These, if they are of ninety-day duration, are the promise by one party to pay a specified sum to another party in ninety days' time. If the status of the accepting institution of a bill is such that the promise to pay is undoubted (i.e. guaranteed) the bill may be sold in the money market for a sum less than the stated total. The difference is the purchaser's profit margin

Fig 2.3 Will your supplier provide the product on suitable credit terms?
Source: Leyland Daf

against which must be set the financial return obtainable elsewhere in the money market. This is bill discounting and it will be seen that the accepting bank has in effect provided security for the funds and not the funds themselves, and it does this for a fee. The borrower is provided with the net proceeds of the discounted bill and has to repay in full at the due date, while the acquiring business house recoups its outlay at the time of repayment. It will be seen that the merchant bank will satisfy itself that the borrower is reliable and that the funds are indeed capable of being recouped. The discount house will itself have borrowed the money from the market.

(Note that bills of exchange are also used in export/import transactions, often under schemes which link them with the documents of title to the goods. The bills are then accepted if the requirements of the deal are met, as outlined in the terms of the contract.)

Debentures

You will appreciate that borrowing frequently involves the commitment of assets of the company as security.

A formal acknowledgement of loan indebtedness is called a debenture. It may or may not include a charge on the borrowing company's assets and it may or may not be under seal.

A prudent lender will always ensure that such a level of borrowing is authorised under the Memorandum and Articles of the company seeking the loan.

There are various types of debenture and a common one is a mortgage on land. There are debentures with a fixed charge on specific property which the borrower may not diminish or sell without the express authority of the debenture holder.

There are also debentures with a floating charge which is an equitable charge on the assets of the borrowing company which may vary in the course of business. If the borrowing company ceases to trade, a floating charge converts to fixed at that time.

It is possible for debentures to be offered to the public in a similar way to the issue of shares.

Factoring

If you employ the services of a factor you exclusively contract with a specialist company to take over the control of, and responsibility for, the collection of all of your invoices: i.e. credit sale proceeds.

At its least it should provide an efficiency of service which yields cash to you more quickly than you can yourself achieve. In its widest form, and at a greater level of cost, it can involve you in exchanging all of your invoices, and receiving, say, 80 per cent of the total value straight away. Clearly there are potential administrative and overhead cost savings whilst any degree of quicker reimbursement is cost effective on a running overdraft.

Fig 2.4 If you sell overseas you should perhaps consider export factoring
Source: Stena Sealink

Whether or not this is a solution for you is a matter for individual examination of the costs and benefits; scale may be very relevant.

Total security for you does not arise unless you have specially contracted for it as a form of bad debt insurance, subject to agreed limits.

Factoring has a further appeal in export transactions where a wider experience of a given market may be of great benefit to the intending exporter.

(*For a detailed consideration of factoring, turn to the case study section.*)

Finance houses

These are specialist providers of finance, particularly in funding the purchase of items of plant and equipment through the operation of hire purchase, or leasing (see below). Their security is usually confined to the asset itself.

The clearing banks have their own finance houses so direct contact from a local bank branch enquiry is easily made for at least one potential alternative source of funding.

(*For a detailed consideration of a finance house, turn to the case study section.*)

Hire purchase

This may sound familiar to most. Under a specially drawn up agreement the consumer is able to acquire goods but to spread the purchase cost over a period. A deposit will be payable and interest is levied and added to the cost; the longer the period involved, the higher the cost of interest charges, and the ownership of the item involved does not pass to the purchaser until every payment has been made. It is likely to be a convenient way of buying smaller plant and equipment where, typically, the supplier has a prepared scheme.

Fig 2.5 A finance house might help to fund a purchase of plant and equipment

On completion of the payment period the ownership passes to the purchaser. This will clearly be an advantage where the item acquired has a realisable value.

(*For large purchases, see Leasing.*)

Leasing

Leasing is concerned with the purchase of new equipment where cash flow prevents outright purchase and it is judged to be appropriate to link this long-term financial commitment to the equally long-term capital items acquired rather than try to involve the shorter-term bank overdraft alternative.

You will have a choice of schemes and there is the possibility that the supplier will have something to offer with training or maintenance benefits; keen to move their products they may also be more flexible in their approach.

Fig 2.6 Many aircraft are leased these days – such as this Virgin A340
Source: Virgin Atlantic

It will be tempting to take on a more expensive machine than you really need; on the other hand, it may bring within reach a more economical, more efficient piece of equipment. On these issues you are likely to be judged if you seek other finance for other purposes.

Your accountant may have a view on tax-timing benefits and may want to point out balance sheet disadvantages, be prepared to seek further financial advice.

You will aim to extend the life of the lease as far as possible through the expected life of the equipment and then judge whether it is likely to have any real value. If it is, a lease purchase or operating lease (e.g. for cars) is preferable. This is because, unlike hire purchase, the user is never going to become the owner. However, at the end of a lease it is usually possible to continue leasing at a nominal rent.

Fig 2.7 It is common for a car, like this Rover 600, to be leased by a company
Source: Rover Cars

Long-term borrowing

This is finance provided over a period of perhaps six or more years up to twenty-five or thirty, usually for major plant or property acquisitions. It will normally be provided under a commercial mortgage (see that section) and may be offered entirely separately from a business's general banking arrangements. A range of banks may be a source and so are some building societies. With long-term borrowing it may be possible to fix an interest rate or to otherwise vary the repayment programme to suit your particular needs.

Start investigating

Take a holiday! You might well come across a loan scheme which offers a 'repayment holiday'. Explain such a feature.

A repayment holiday _____

_____

_____

_____

Mergers and take-overs

Usually a take-over relates to the acquiring of one business by a stronger business in the same type of trade, or by a strong business pursuing a policy of diversification. Mergers may represent the combining of more or less equal businesses for economy of scale and are a joint decision.

A management buy-out occurs when insiders (existing staff) acquire a business or a division of a business. It will be common here for extra funding to be sought and this will be more likely to flow from existing banking connections if the key personnel are known and approved.

On a large scale, mergers and take-overs require the specialist services of a merchant bank. In a contested take-over the merchant bank will be very active and fees will rise accordingly. If there is no contention, the advice may be limited to the price agreement.

If the take-over involves the acquisition of a business which is then closed, and the trade, the plant and the premises all disposed of, this is an act of 'asset stripping'.

Overseeing the largest operations of this kind, and with a power of veto, is the Monopolies and Mergers Commission. There are rules compelling an interest to be made known publicly if a certain level of shareholding is reached.

Overdrafts

These are an agreed extent of borrowing from your bank and are primarily regarded as short term but, subject to satisfactory annual review and adjustment, tend to become in practice a more permanent feature of trading by many business ventures. They have advantages of ease of arrangement and cost effectiveness, as you only pay interest on the actual overdraft amount which is likely to fluctuate from day to day.

Bankers will wish to have security for their lending and they will fix a price according to their assessment of the risk. You may be asked to give a personal guarantee. The interest rate fixed will be a given percentage expressed as an addition to the general base rate. Then, whilst the base rate fluctuates, the total interest is readily identifiable and remains currently appropriate without the need to renegotiate it. Sometimes there will be an overall minimum rate which would apply even though a falling base rate would otherwise call for a reduction. (LIBOR may occasionally be used as an alternative to base rate.)

The interest is assessed daily and charged monthly or quarterly to your account. You will almost certainly have had to compile a cash flow forecast (*see Business loans*).

Always bear in mind the fact that the bank may at any time revise its policy and require a reduction or even a total repayment without warning.

(*See also Security for borrowing.*)

Security for borrowing

Every business has a collection of assets, and its balance sheet will set out the most basic of details in two categories, current assets and fixed assets.

Current assets are those which are involved with the direct trading activities of the company and they range from cash and book debts to stocks of materials, work in progress and finished goods. They are by their nature constantly fluctuating, but they are capable of providing security in general terms by what is termed a floating charge (*and see Debentures on page 44*).

If there is no security available from the current or fixed resources of the company it may be necessary for a principal to provide his personal guarantee backed by his personal property.

Fixed assets include:

- Premises – freehold / leasehold
- Plant
- Machinery
- Equipment / furniture
- Vehicles

These are, by their nature, not readily convertible into cash but all have a realisable value. Some, subject in emergency or in liquidation to immediate sale, would yield much less than their stated value. The list is in descending order of difficulty of liquidising – cash raising.

For extra details of the items themselves you may turn to a company's Annual Report, where notes to the accounts may show how annual depreciation has been charged to reduce original costs to the present levels shown.

Share issues

Shares coupled with membership rights of the holders are the financial life-blood of the commercial world enabling businesses to expand and investors to have a wide choice of investment, flexibility of fund management and a degree of control over the management of the company.

An existing company will have issued shares on its inception. A widening of share holdings may come about at a later stage by:

1 Issuing more shares to existing members only at a price attractive to them.

2 Issuing shares to the public at a set price at a particular time.

The latter is a major financial operation and the main aid will be a merchant bank. The shares may be 'over subscribed' (demand exceeding the available quantity of shares), and in this case proportional allocations will have to be worked out. If they are 'under subscribed' it will be expected that the merchant bank will have arranged for an underwriter to take up the surplus. A share issue must be supported by a prospectus drawn up by accountants.

Ordinary shares form the main part of share capital and the holders have rights to speak and vote at general meetings and to receive dividends. The dividend is variable according to profitability and the commitments of the company.

Preference shares have a fixed rate of interest and holders have less rights than ordinary shareholders, but do take preference when payment of interest arises. A company may decide not to pay a dividend but it cannot decide to pay a dividend on ordinary shares unless preference shareholders have been satisfied first.

Short-term borrowing

We need look no further here than the overdraft arranged with your bank which is usually secured in some way. A bank offering short-term funding will normally make the facility available for up to twelve months, but this will depend on individual circumstances. Your cash flow forecast will indicate your needs.

Start-up capital

You are aiming to get a business started and you will find that the banks have special staff terms and schemes specially designed to help you.

For this purpose you will be assured to have a potentially sound business idea and a plan for its operation. This means that you have a real prospect of satisfying customers at the right price.

You will need to judge the scale of your enterprise and you will need a cash flow.

They may offer:

- a start-up loan at advantageous rates
- a development loan, possibly long term
- an overdraft.

You may be under some pressure or possibly an obligation to take up some insurance covers which they promote, perhaps in a useful combined form.

(*See Venture capital, and also Business advice from your bank, in Section C.*)

Stock exchanges

The stock exchange in the City of London is not unique. There are others throughout the world. The London Exchange is the third largest

Fig 2.8 The New York stock exchange, located on Wall Street, is the largest securities exchange in the world
R.Marlow-photographer, K.Vincent-pilot

after the USA and Japan. Stock exchanges are markets for the shares of companies and government bonds (gilts), and the introduction of automation has effectively reduced the importance of the actual trading premises themselves so that dealers no longer make direct personal contact 'on the floor'. Dealers who handle the transactions have to be members.

Settlement of all transactions used to be programmed into two-week periods known as 'accounts'. The main stock exchanges in the USA and in Japan have more frequent settlements, and over the next few years the London Exchange will have shortened its settlement period dramatically.

In June 1995 the London Exchange introduced a five-day rolling settlement process, having operated a ten-day system since July 1994. The long-term aim is to settle transactions in just three days.

The Alternative Investment Market (AIM)

Newly created and opened in June 1995, this is a stock exchange initiative aimed at smaller companies seeking investment capital and venture capitalists seeking smaller companies, often with a greater risk element.

The new market recognises the difficulty often met by smaller companies at this stage of their development and it will expect to act as a stepping stone to later full public trading on the exchange itself.

Whilst this is an entirely new venture it is to be noted that the Unlisted Securities Market is to close at the end of 1996.

To join AIM a company must prepare a prospectus which gives a detailed picture of the business and must nominate an adviser. The adviser may be a London Exchange member; if not, a nominated broker from that membership will also be required. (Other possible advisers are other brokers, a lawyer, banker, accountant or other financial professional.)

The adviser and broker will be a permanent feature as continuity will be necessary to avoid risk of cancellation.

Once a company has entered the market its share price, and other information such as its profits and turnover, will be available through SEATS (Stock Exchange Alternative Trading Service), which is a computerised trading system used by stockbrokers.

 ### *Start investigating*

Watch out for articles in the press on companies entering the market and retain these.

Remember that buyers of shares should be aware that the potential high rates of return on such investments are matched by a high degree of risk.

Venture capital

This, along with LINC, involves funding which has been dealt with under Business angels, but under this heading you will find funding which flows from institutions such as

- pension funds
- insurance companies
- development agencies
- banks
- venture capitalists
- insurance companies

as well as from individuals.

Here you will be required to provide ordinary shares in your company and the fund will probably be looking to growth towards a flotation; a directorship for the investor is also a likely condition.

You will be sure to be critically investigated and you may well require expert advice.

Venture capital is targeted at the entrepreneurial enterprise.

Start investigating

Assess the characteristics of a typical entrepreneur and judge why this may be an appropriate scheme in this instance.

Working capital

This is the day-to-day funding which you require to bridge the gap between your outgoings and incomings – the period during which you are 'out of pocket' having laid out monies for goods or materials and are awaiting the return from sale of the finished article which you have produced.

Most crucially the level of stock you retain will have a considerable bearing and this is not immediately apparent when you consult your cash flow, which was discussed in the opening comments for this section.

Section C

The need for specialist advice and assistance

In this section we will consider the following topics:

- **Actuarial advice**
- **Business advice from your bank**
- **Financial record keeping**
- **Independent financial advice**
- **Internal and external audit**
- **Pensions advice**
- **Stockbroking**
- **Taxation advice**

A business might typically turn to the following for these products and services:

- **Accountants**
- **Actuaries**
- **Business bankers**
- **Company secretary**
- **Financial advisers**
- **Merchant bankers**
- **Stockbrokers**

Actuarial advice

An actuary is a specialist in aiding risk assessment based on his interpretation of detailed statistical data. His advice is commonly provided in insurance and assurance to underwriters who will, with his help, assess risks and fix a price (premium) for the cover. Unless your business is in this field you are unlikely to have direct need for this advice other than for your pension structure. If you aim to establish your own company pension fund for your employees rather than opt for a commercial alternative, you will need the actuary's expert guidance on life expectancy of your workforce in order to judge the right level of funding.

The same applies if you have a merger or take-over involving an existing pension scheme which may or may not be viable in its present form, and this could have a bearing on the overall price for the business. The actuary will also have expertise involving the special pension scheme requirements of directors.

The Government Actuary's Department (GAD) now provides consultancy advice on pensions to fee-paying commercial customers.

(*See also Pensions advice.*)

Business advice from your bank

If starting up, look for the special schemes run by the banks for entirely new enterprises. They will be prepared to offer advice on the running of your business and have a variety of programmes for procedure and financing.

Firstly there are the basic tools for account operation:

- Cheque books
- Paying-in books
- Monthly statements
- Standing orders
- Direct debits
- Business cards

Secondly you will look for a first year with no bank charges provided that:

- The account stays in credit
- The turnover is within a stated limit (e.g. £100,000)
- The frequency of transactions is not excessive

- There are no complex requirements

If the account is not in credit there may be a choice of monthly or quarterly charges for the credit which the bank agrees to provide. Note that there will be penalties if the limit is exceeded.

(See also Start-up capital in Section B.)

For a business which is already functioning you may look to your bank for guidance on:

- Money transfer services
- Short- and long-term finance
- Leasing
- Mortgages
- Taxation
- Pensions
- General insurance business
- Investment
- Market information, domestic and international
- Technology
- Registrar services (shareholding records)
- Documentary storage

Fee-paying services by the bank include:

- Bankers references, i.e. status enquiries (where a range of standard replies cover the extent and quality of the bank's experience of the customer in question)
- Letters to auditors
- Night safe provisions
- Cheque stopping
- Bankers drafts
- Open credit facilities (arrangements at other branches)
- Express cheque clearance

Financial record keeping

You have a legal obligation under company law to maintain proper account records whether they be handwritten in bound books or housed in a complex of computers. For the financial record all such accounts will be relevant but, whatever system you use, you will seek to have quick and easy ways of checking on your:

- current cash position
- debtors
- creditors
- working capital
- stock levels

The records will need to satisfy your accountants (*see Internal and external audit*) as well as the Inland Revenue, National Insurance and VAT inspectors.

In a complex world it is advisable to keep records and systems as simple as possible. A ready-made computer program should be obtainable for most needs, or a handwritten set of books can provide the system. Both can be tailored to cater for individual circumstances.

The system should aim to be:

1 Simple to use, for ease of operation and inspection.

2 Accurate and efficient.

3 Comprehensive but without excess information.

4 Economical to operate.

5 Able to produce key figures promptly.

6 Protective against abuse (e.g. where cash transactions occur).

The government bodies have standard procedures or requirements which must be incorporated into your system and there are penalties for non-compliance.

A basic characteristic of general accounting systems is the feature of 'double entry' which recognises the two sides of any transaction, most easily represented by the 'from' and 'to' identities (or debit and credit).

The fact that, in total, all debits must equal all credits if the transactions have been correctly recorded, offers a useful cross-checking tool which may be repeatedly introduced as a checking aid.

A special record will be kept of your securities. Those which are held at your bank will be listed by them and reported on annually on request to your auditors (*see Audit*). Others, charged elsewhere, will require similar confirmation, while those which are not charged may involve documents of title which are lodged at the bank purely for safe-keeping and can be reported on by them.

Independent financial advice

Sources include:

- Financial advisers
- Consultants
- Accountants – your own or a specialist firm
- Banks or building societies – often via specialist divisions
- Merchant banks
- Solicitors – your own or a specialist firm
- Insurance sales staff and financial advisers
- Chartered surveyors (for property)
- Trade protection organisations
- Confederation of British Industry (CBI)
- Chambers of Commerce
- Enterprise and development agencies
- Actuaries (for pensions)
- Stockbrokers
- Small business associations

The representatives of finance houses and insurance companies are legally constrained by the regulations of LAUTRO (Life Assurance and Unit Trust Regulatory Organisation), while independent financial advisers are authorised by FIMBRA (Financial Intermediaries Managers and Brokers Regulatory Association) or their own professional body. Investment managers are regulated by IMRO (Investment Management Regulatory Organisation).

Surveyors will revalue properties for annual account purposes, will purchase, sell, let property and advise on the economic use of property.

Solicitors will also be needed for all types of property transaction.

Internal and external audit

'Having the auditors in' usually means the annual investigations of the accountancy firm contracted to prepare and publish your annual accounts. By arrangement they may make interim visits to your head office and your branches. These are your external auditors and are independent. Internal audit is a planned vetting carried out by your own appointed staff for routine or special reasons and, as employees, are not independent. Both will seek a true record of transactions, will expect accuracy and completeness of records; entries of incoming and outgoing cash must be capable of checking against approved invoices or similar documents ('vouchers').

There are new developments in this field. Small companies (turnover below £90,000 per annum) are exempt from audit, while those in the range of £90,000 – £350,000 must now provide an independent accountant's 'compilation report' which must confirm that the accounts are in accordance with statutory requirements and have been prepared from the company's accounting records.

The emphasis turns to the directors' responsibilities for setting accounting policies, choosing suitable record systems, keeping the records, preventing and detecting fraud and irregularities and providing 'a true and fair view' of the business affairs.

In practice the board of directors will often rely on their Company Secretary who has a general responsibility for legal compliance and through whose office the routine official demands and deadlines will be channelled.

Fig 2.9 A team of auditors will be sent into larger companies

It should be noted that the Companies Acts stipulate that the directors of all companies must appoint a Company Secretary: the company itself is a separate legal entity which can only function through its appointed officials.

This applies regardless of the scale of the business, ranging from the smallest private company to public companies. Not all of the latter are 'floated' for public share ownership despite the name.

Auditors have full regard for the special requirements of the inspectors of HM Customs and Excise (for VAT), the Inland Revenue (for Corporation Tax and PAYE) and National Insurance (for employees' contributions and benefits), and the routine visits by these inspectors provide a further level of record checking. The inspectors have considerable powers.

The internal auditors will also be expected to monitor and modify the company's systems for most accurate, efficient and reliable methods of operation. Their detailed knowledge should enable them to carry out cross-checks to detect irregularities.

The external auditor will be subject to a combination of statutory and established professional rules and guidelines. He must issue a report to accompany the annual filed accounts of the company. You will hope for a report which is not 'qualified', that is, where there are no stated reservations or doubts about any aspects of the accounts or the assets and their valuations. (Occasionally auditors will have to issue a qualifying comment for purely technical reasons.)

Your bank will be approached by auditors for formal confirmation of bank balances on your accounts at the end of your financial year and for a list of securities held by them in your name. The bank will charge for this and will include any documents of title merely retained by them for safekeeping on your instructions.

Annual accounts

The balance sheet entries of amounts for reserves and the profit and loss account reveal the extent of profits retained in the business.

Accounts are further formalised and standardised by the compliance with Statements of Standard Accounting Practice (SSAPs) which accountancy firms are required to follow in practice, though they do not have legal force. One of these covers a statement of Source and Application of Funds which enlarges on balance sheet information and will reveal the yearly increase or decrease in working capital.

Pensions advice

This guidance is needed by employers seeking to provide pension benefits for their employees over and above the levels provided by the state. Their scheme may be

- contributory (the employee pays a set proportion from salary), or
- non-contributory (the employer pays in full),

and the level of benefit might lead to 'contracting out' of the State Earnings Related Pension Scheme (SERPS). The company will choose either to operate its own fund, employing trustees for its management, or to arrange for an insurance company to provide a suitable scheme. Advice on choosing between these alternatives will most readily come from your accountants or an independent adviser.

If an 'in-house' scheme is planned you will seek actuarial advice to ensure that the scope of the provision is sufficient to meet the expected needs of the beneficiaries. At its simplest, an ageing workforce will involve early withdrawals from the fund.

In company commercial schemes you will be able to rely on the LAUTRO regulations (*see Advisers*) to ensure that you are actually comparing yields on the same basis of calculation (*see also Actuarial advice*).

Stockbroking

Stockbrokers purchase and sell shares and government securities which are marketed by the stock exchanges and they charge a fee based on the sums of money involved.

They also provide investment advice involving shares and bonds and they will offer further guidance on share flotations (new issues), but you will expect to use the services of a merchant bank for this purpose.

Many brokers in the City of London will look to the Reuters screen on their desk as an essential piece of equipment, providing a range of facts and figures, including the latest news, share prices and currency rates.

Reuters is a world renowned news source supplying the media, but it also uses its resources to provide financial information flowing from the impact of the news items, by instant electronic means direct to organisations involved in the financial markets. An example of how this works in practice was given by the 1991 Soviet coup attempt. Along with the most prompt reporting of the coup itself (and, subsequently, its collapse) they produced economic updates on UK treasury bill yields, Soviet gas oil prices, Frankfurt Stock Exchange reactions and currency rates.

Taxation advice

This may be provided by your accountants, specialist sections of commercial banks, merchant banks, other financiers or independent specialists.

The aim will be for you to take advantage of the taxation system within the legal framework and will involve both the way you arrange your affairs and the timing. This is always in terms of legitimate business planning and never of tax evasion.

Accountants

Your company appoints auditors and you have seen under the section on audits the importance of the annual accounts and the report by accountants which must accompany them.

From the close involvement necessary for the compilation and approval of the accounts, the accountant develops a detailed knowledge of your business and is, therefore, in an excellent position to advise you or to represent you in your quest for financial support.

This technical expertise is readily geared to your needs and abilities in financial accounting and management, taxation and audit.

Actuaries

These are specialists functioning primarily in the insurance risk sector. (*See Actuarial advice, page 58.*)

Business bankers

They comprise the specialists working for both the commercial banks and the merchant banks.

Company Secretary

The Companies Acts stipulate that each company must have an appointed official named and filed at Companies House as a Company Secretary. This is the only specified official in addition to directors of the company which, as a separate legal entity, has a special status of its own.

The Company Secretary is appointed by the Board of Directors and attends and regulates their meetings, ensuring that they operate within the powers laid down by Companies Acts and other legislation and within the company's own Memorandum and Articles of Association. These are sets of rules and standards filed by the company and thus make clear to any enquirer the objects of the company and the way it chooses to operate (within the law as provided by statute).

The Company Secretary will look after the statutory books of the company and will keep its Register of Members, unless the public scale of the business requires the services of a registrar and a separate special department.

Qualification will be determined by the status of the company: private or public. Not all public companies (PLCs) are subject to share transactions in stock exchanges or the new AIM market.

In the smallest companies the Company Secretary may not need formal qualification and the company may rely on the services of its solicitor or accountant for the strict compliance with filed returns and accounts.

Financial advisers

Financial advisers are to be found within the business banks, the accountancy sector and as independent professionals.

Merchant banks

These are a main source of major finance and financial advice and, whilst many have an illustrious history, there are others which have developed as extensions of general banks. They borrow from the money market or direct from investors and lay much store on personal contact and assessment. Their support is usually vital in the flotation of new shares and conversion to public from private company, and they also play a large role in take-overs, especially where the basis is a bid which is regarded as hostile by the target. They advise on all formal credit, fund management, investment and assurance services. Merchant banks which put their names to bills of exchange are known as *accepting houses*.

Stockbrokers

Stockbrokers facilitate the purchase and sale of shares on stock exchanges and offer expert advice on investment opportunities.

Section D

The need to transfer money

In this section we will consider the following topics:

- **Automated payments**
- **Business accounts**
- **Business credit and charge cards**
- **Cash management**
- **CHAPS**
- **Currency payments**
- **Exchanging currencies**
- **Fundsflow**
- **International payments**
- **Money transmission**

A business might typically turn to the following for these products and services:

- **Bankers Automated Clearing Services (BACS)**
- **Clearing banks**
- **Charge card issuers**
- **Credit card issuers**
- **Foreign banks**
- **Mondex UK Ltd**
- **Merchant banks**
- **SWIFT (The Society for Worldwide Interbank Financial Telecommunication)**

You are trading so you will be purchasing goods and services and all of these have to be paid for before supply, at the point of supply, after supply, or a mixture of these according to the terms which you have agreed.

In some instances you will be particularly concerned with the security of your funds to ensure that they are released only when ownership in the goods has clearly and definitely passed to you. Usually this will equate to possession of the goods by you i.e. off-loaded into your warehouse, for instance.

It will be the function of your accounts department to handle and document the actual transfer, ensuring that sufficient funds exist for payments and that efficient use is made of receipts. The department will be guided by the bank requirements which will include the authorising signatures of designated directors (usually those on mandate to the bank who are cheque signatories).

Speed of transfer is something we can usually take for granted, but there may be particular circumstances where payment must be in a certain form and at a certain place at a certain time, and this may require special planning and provision.

Automated payments

BACS

BACS stands for Bankers Automated Clearing Services and building society accounts are also included in the system. Automated payments are made by electronic means via an automated clearing house. Originally introduced to provide a method to cope with fund transfers between the banks, this system has been developed to handle customers' direct transfers originating as (commonly, regular monthly) credit transfer or direct debit authorities, all without the need to generate any additional paperwork over and above the initial instruction. You may wish to use BACS to handle, for example, the payment of salaries to your employees, or to cover your water rates.

Business accounts

These encompass the basic bank provisions of current and call (deposit) accounts as well as some more specialist facilities. On the current accounts you may expect to pay a small standing charge of, say, £10.00 per quarter and a further charge for every entry on the statement (say 60p). Statements will usually be issued to you monthly and you will, as an accounting operation, expect to reconcile them with your own cash book record. This will be done by

- taking the cash book balance agreed a month ago (the opening balance),
- adding the receipts recorded since then,
- deducting the purchases recorded since then, to provide a closing balance,
- then adjusting for cheque payments recorded by you but not yet presented at your bank, and
- adjusting for any receipt recorded but not at the bank or vice versa,

to arrive at the bank's total.

You will open a business account with the support of a *mandate,* which instructs the bank on such issues as your approved personnel authorised to sign cheques, deal with securities and release documents on behalf of your business.

Business credit and charge cards

A business charge card from your bank is a useful tool for a host of day-to-day purchases including travel (tickets, hotels, fuel), sundries and cash (including local currencies abroad). Unlike the personal credit card there is no option of instalment payment, but there is a monthly statement, the full total of which is charged to your company account shortly after you receive it. Cash is subject to interest charges from the date of the withdrawal.

The monthly statement is a useful account document as it conveniently summarises a range of regular outgoings in a form readily absorbed by accounting or auditing staff or inspectors. This is pertinent because the likely uses of the card cover categories most frequently scrutinised.

Cash management

In all businesses it is vital that the management keep track of the balances of all the company accounts. In a large company different accounts at bank branches throughout the country (or even the world) are totalled up in terms of debit and credit totals, to give an overall funding picture. The purpose of sound cash management is to ensure that no significant surplus is left uninvested or no major funding shortfall exists. In complex situations many large organisations seek a sophisticated cash management facility from their bankers.

Cash management is an electronic service which is specially geared to providing you with up-to-the-minute details of account balances and information for forecasting (compare with the traditional cash flow). It may be seen that such information improves your ability to use funds to the greatest advantage and it includes updating on the cheques

Fig 2.10 Many banks are able to provide up to date account information direct to a terminal in your office

which are in the process of the normal three-day clearance procedure – all linked into your personal computer.

Thus you may have immediate displays to show end-of-day balance, next day's credits of cheques paid in and due for clearance (third day of clearance system and a 'one-day float' in terms of closeness to realising in your favour), BACS credits and automated standing orders arriving but deducting your cheques presented, your direct debit and standing order payments.

CHAPS

The Clearing House Automated Payments System enables banks to transfer large payments instantly (i.e. same day) by computer link rather than telephone transfer. The paying bank initiates the transfer which is complete when the receiving bank electronically responds. The paying bank also guarantees its contribution, i.e. provides cleared funds, and because of this it may exercise caution in the operation of the system. To pay by this method you may face a fee of up to £20.

These are also known as *fundsflow transfers*.

Start investigating

Consider the following situation:

Your college or school wishes to pay £30,000 to a computer supplier, and it is agreed that a CHAPS transfer will be initiated for £10,000 immediately to enable the installation to proceed quickly.

Complete the following details. Some of the facts will be genuine; others you will have to complete on a theoretical basis.

1 Paying bank _____

2 Originator _____

3 Beneficiary _____

4 Payee bank _____

5 Sort code (a) Paying bank _____

(b) Payee bank _____

Currency payments

In dealing, through your bank, with the foreign exchange market you are concerned with purchases which are either:

- **spot** – immediately required at the current exchange rate, or are pitched, or
- **forward** – perhaps one, two or three months ahead of requirement (or further by arrangement).

Thanks to modern technology the market is world-wide.

(*See also International payments on page 76.*)

Start investigating

Where can you easily discover the exchange rates for the major currencies? Give two sources:

1 _____

2 _____

What is the present rate of exchange for the following selection of currencies (against sterling)?

1 US Dollar _____

2 Deutschmark _____

3 Japanese Yen _____

Select a further two major currencies and record them below:

1 _____   _____

2 _____   _____

(All the above rates applied on   /   / 1 9   )

Exchanging currencies

Most of the major banks will provide a range of foreign currency services.

(*See also Section A – Foreign currency management, and International payments below.*)

Fundsflow

(*See CHAPS on page 74.*)

International payments

There is ever-increasing provision in the world's financial centres for currency payments to be made, but the main flows of purchases and sales are in

- US Dollars
- Japanese Yen
- Pounds Sterling
- Swiss Francs
- German Deutschmarks

for reasons of stability, size of economy, traditional use, and general acceptability. This means that money markets buy and sell quantities of these currencies whether or not they are directly involved in any particular transactions and will commonly supply them 'forward' for one, two, or three months. This will protect you from any adverse market movement weakening your own or strengthening the required currency, *and* you will have achieved a certain level of commitment.

If this is just one of a series of such payments by you in one or a range of currencies you will need staff skilled in the market and will lay down or give the staff strict guidelines for their operating. The operation will be more complex in the quite likely event that you are receiving currency payments as well as making them.

As a receiver of payments from abroad, you will not have the same protection against market changes but if you are in a position to match receipts against expenditures you will have achieved a greater level of security.

The market is used by speculators in a given currency, occasionally with spectacular results.

SWIFT (The Society for Worldwide Interbank Financial Telecommunication) has for many years provided a computer link between all the banks of the trading nations of the world, displacing airmail transfers and telex transfers, as the modern rapid way to move funds globally.

For more modest purposes a payment abroad by your own cheque is possible if contract and conditions allow, but the receiver must then lodge it with his bank for collection, and there are delays and expenses which make this an undesirable method. The foreign supplier will much prefer a cheque drawn in currency on a bank and account in their country, or in sterling (requiring conversion). The bank's cheque is known as a *banker's draft*.

When you investigate the ways payments can be made overseas, you may also consider the following:

- bills of exchange
- documentary credits
- Eurocheques
- plastic cards
- travellers cheques.

Bills of exchange are also used in export/import transactions, often with title documents giving the buyer the right to the goods at the agreed point (ex works, ex port, ex ship etc.).

Documentary credits are used in the payment of imports/exports. They set out the requirements to be met for payment to be made.

A bill of exchange may be involved and the requirements all relate to the precise nature of the documents covering the consignment.

Eurocheques supported by a Eurocheque card enable the traveller to write cheques in the local currency of the country in question drawn on the home bank account and subject to conversion to sterling at a rate applicable on the day of payment.

Credit and charge cards (i.e. 'plastics') have cash drawing functions abroad, and are widely accepted in many retail outlets and at hotels and restaurants.

Fig 2.11 International trade will typically involve complex documentation
Source: Stena Sealink

Travellers cheques in sterling or foreign currency are widely accepted and are more secure than local currency or sterling. By opting for the currency of the country in question the user is able to avoid any subsequent adverse exchange rate movements.

Money transmission

The banks have their own quick and efficient computer-linked transfer services such as National Westminster's 'Business Line' and 'Bank Line', and 'LloydsLink' and 'Bank Option', which transmit through CHAPS to accounts at other banks or to other accounts at the same bank. They are quick and reliable and easy to use.

When considering automated transfers it is worth comparing the standard cheque clearing programme:

Day 1 You receive a cheque and you pay it into your bank for credit to your account.

Day 2 The cheque reaches your bank head office, goes via the clearing house to the head office of the bank on which it is drawn, and is sent out from there to the branch which holds the account on which it is drawn.

Day 3 The cheque reaches the branch holding the drawer's account where it is either met, if funds suffice, or is rejected and returned to sender, where it will cancel the Day 1 credit.

This three-day cycle has recently started to look rather outdated as more and more transfers have been made electronically. Many banks are considering *truncation*, which at least halts the physical movement of cheques around the nation, with electronic messages ensuring the correct parties are credited and debited. In reality this is only a partial solution as Electronic Data Interchange (EDI) is the potential solution to efficient money transmission and much more. EDI involves the linking of a supplier's computer system with its customers and bankers so that a delivery of goods automatically generates an invoice and appropriate payment. With such a system cheques are clearly an awkward irrelevance. (*See also BACS* (page 71) *and SWIFT* (page 77).)

Clearing banks

The clearing banks are so called because they all belong to the Bankers' Clearing House in the City of London and thus have direct interchange of cheque-clearing operations. It is often thought that they comprise just the 'Big Four' –

- Barclays
- National Westminster
- Midland
- Lloyds

– but this is not so. The Bank of England is itself a major member and it is the holder of the account of each other member to facilitate the daily movements. Others include the Co-op (Co-operative Bank) and TSB (Trustee Savings Bank).

British bankers have their own trade association, The British Bankers' Association, based in Lombard Street in the City of London, which includes all the major banks and many foreign-owned or foreign-controlled banks, and this body is involved in government regulations, business and banking law, European Community issues, securities regulation, the money markets, and much more.

Major companies do not have access to the Banking Ombudsman, but sole traders and partnerships do. The scope of the Ombudsman is limited and you cannot complain of quality of advice, only of something going wrong and causing you an injustice, e.g. a bank's failure to move funds to your advantage in spite of instructions to do so.

Mondex UK Ltd

The Mondex payments scheme was launched in July 1995 as an alternative to cash.

(*See Case Study on page 121.*)

The need to protect against risks

In this section we will consider the following topics:

- **Risk management**
- **Insurable risks**
- **Non-insurable risks**
- **Insurance services**
- **London International Financial Futures & Options Exchange (LIFFE)**

A business might typically turn to the following for these products and services:

- **Assurance companies**
- **Clearing banks**
- **Insurance brokers**
- **Insurance companies**
- **LIFFE**
- **Lloyd's brokers**

Risk management

You are concerned to protect your business in the event of mishap. It is not sufficient that your premises and contents are themselves insured in the event of severe fire damage if you have not taken out insurance to cover the business interruption (consequential loss), costs of temporary accommodation, production delays, contracting work out, breach of contract, extra overheads.

Internal management will probably be handled or overseen by the Company Secretary who will have a general knowledge of insurance matters extending to both the operations of the business and the welfare and protection of its employees. Much of the protection will arise through employment and other legislation which may involve inspections: there will be issues concerning protection of confidential information both operative and personal, all requiring careful attention.

All insurance is based on the requirement that cover has been obtained with 'utmost good faith', meaning that no withholding of information in the proposal details has occurred by which the underwriter could have been misled. (This is to be contrasted with the approach to general contract where 'let the buyer beware' sums up the basic agreement.)

Having decided on the business risks you wish to insure (*see Insurable risks*) you will need to assess their cost and see whether any savings are possible by:

1 Fuller compliance with requirements, such as the fitting of more sophisticated alarm systems against fire and theft.

2 Partial bearing of the risk. This might be appropriate if you enhance your debtor control, and feel that you need to ensure against non-payment to a lesser extent.

3 Reducing the cover, perhaps because a change in your level of business has lessened the need for protection in other areas.

4 Changing your insurer(s). You may be able to find a more competitive quote elsewhere, from specialist providers, or alternatively, by taking a wide-ranging package of protection from an individual insurer.

In addition to the risks for which the insurance industry provides protection, there are the everyday risks of the commercial world and these include unforeseen trade fluctuations for a wide variety of reasons from flood and earthquake to politically inspired embargo.

You are also vulnerable to inadequate or dishonest advice and dealings, some of which will be mitigated by the intervention of a regulatory body.

You will be better prepared if you keep up to date with the national and international developments which are reported in the press and you always seek to obtain advice from more than one source.

Insurable risks

You can take out an insurance cover if you are facing a monetary loss in the event of a mishap: this is called an *insurable risk*. *Insurance* protects against events which *may* happen; *assurance* provides cover for events which *will* happen. (Assurance therefore applies to whole life cover as death is a certainty.)

The premium is assessed by an underwriter with the expert assessment of an actuary, who will have comprehensive statistical information which will lead to a clear indication of the degree of risk. In the case of life assurance this expertise is concerned with all of the factors involved in measuring the life expectancy of the applicant.

Fig 2.12 A variety of risks will need to be covered

Insurable risks commonly include:

- Fire
- Theft
- Employer's liability
- Public liability
- Consequential loss (business interruption)
- Construction (contractor's all risks)
- Credit (bad debts)
- Engineering/Marine/Motor
- Life/Injury/Sickness/Key person
- Professional indemnity
- Legal expenses
- Pollution.

It is increasingly common for rules to be laid down by the insurer aiming to reduce the risk. For example:

- Locks and security devices combat theft.
- Building construction, extinguishers, sprinklers, approved storage and use of combustible materials help to prevent or to reduce the extent of fire damage.

Property is insured for the cost of rebuilding, including costs of site clearance and architects' fees, and not for market value which may be higher or lower. If you are a lessee you will seek to have your interest noted on the policy and to ensure that the property would be restored after serious damage.

You may expect inspections to check that these are carried out and a leasing company might have its own conditions in respect of the equipment it is leasing to you.

 ## *Start investigating*

As you investigate insurance issues you may discover that it is a legal requirement for a business to have insurance cover in respect of certain risks.

Note such examples shown here when you become aware of them. Legally a business must have insurance cover for:

_____

_____

_____

_____

_____

Non-insurable risks

You cannot insure where you do not have an insurable interest (*see page 83*) and there are subjects which are not insurable. Some risks which are exceptional in character or scale might not be accepted by general insurers but could be covered at Lloyd's, which aims to be truly comprehensive for anyone having an insurable interest. You cannot insure against economic charges (e.g. taxation), or most commercial losses through a fall in demand, or your own misjudgement, or for equipment wear and tear.

Insurance services

General insurance covers the various subjects listed above under insurable risks.

Life assurance covers the whole life or a given period (endowment) on completion of which the payment is made.

Key person insurance protects the business in the event of the loss of certain key personnel, whether by incapacity or death. The impact might be more severe for the smaller business with loss of profit, extra expense and possible problems over loan security.

Pensions insurance is taken up by employers who do not wish to operate a pension fund of their own. There is a wide range of specialist insurance companies which compete with the major ones, or aim to offer protection for highly specific market niches.

Sickness and *critical illness covers* provide respectively for medical costs and lump-sum payments, while *permanent health insurance* protects against loss of income due to illness or disability.

(*A highly detailed study of insurance services is presented in the case study section of this text.*)

London International Financial Futures & Options Exchange (LIFFE)

Trading in financial futures and options originated in the USA. Membership extends to banks, brokers and discount houses and the trade is in currencies, stocks and shares and interest rate contracts and options. It aims to protect any organisation faced with a fixed future commitment and vulnerable to price fluctuations in the interim.

Trading is by traditional method 'in the pit' which is the section of the market on the floor of the exchange and is done by what is termed 'open outcry', combining shouting and hand signals between traders. An open palm-forward raised hand identifies a seller, while the back of the open hand is displayed by a prospective buyer.

The London Exchange was opened in 1982, and growth has been considerable. In October 1993 10 million contracts in a month was exceeded for the first time. In April 1995 average daily volume was 440,989 contracts, and average daily turnover £111 billion.

The ruling body, the Securities and Investment Board (SIB), is the chief regulator of UK financial services and surveillance is carried out. Powers of suspension, levying fines on member firms and individual traders, and expulsion, are employed if need be.

Assurance companies

These are the Life specialists. They include 'mutual' companies where the ownership is in the hands of the policy holders, not shareholders. Profit then stays in the fund and boosts the eventual proceeds to the insured. They will insure the whole life and will be very active in pension scheme provisions.

 ## *Start investigating*

Life assurance: watch out for adverts in the daily papers by assurance companies offering their products. Whenever you see an appropriate promotion complete the grid below:

	Company name	*Product name*
1	_____	_____
2	_____	_____
3	_____	_____

Clearing banks

Nowadays, clearing banks provide a complete range of insurance products, and they have staff trained in the subject to advise their customers. This is, of course, backed by the widest business experience, as well as specific knowledge of an individual company.

Insurance brokers

Insurance brokers are the intermediaries for your acquisition of insurance cover when you are not dealing direct with the insurance company. They include Lloyd's brokers who are approved to deal direct with the underwriters at Lloyd's.

In insurance business the term 'agent' is in practice applied to other businessmen who are most commonly professionals in another field who have, through their contacts, an ability to generate insurance business, which they then pass to brokers or insurers for formal completion.

Insurance companies

Insurance companies may offer a range of general insurance covers or may specialise. You may reach them direct or through an insurance broker. Prominent examples of general insurance companies include:

- Commercial Union
- Eagle Star
- General Accident
- Guardian Royal Exchange
- Legal and General
- Norwich Union
- Pearl
- Prudential
- Royal
- Sun Alliance

(*For a detailed consideration of the insurance industry turn to the case study section.*)

 ## *Start investigating*

Watch out for these companies advertising on the television or in the press. To supplement your portfolio you may wish to retain details of products advertised by these providers, or others which are also in the market.

Lloyd's brokers

It is the claim of Lloyd's of London that almost anything can be insured there and they often provide cover unobtainable elsewhere. Its origins from coffee house meetings three hundred years ago are well known, but its size and scope today are very considerable. The risk is borne by members grouped in syndicates with guiding underwriters. The broker will approach those which specialise in your type of risk and will arrange the cover you require. Lloyd's brokers alone may do this, and they are specially approved by Lloyd's.

Start investigating

Changes at Lloyd's. Over the last few years the Lloyd's market has undergone considerable change. New practices and schemes are being considered to allow the market to respond to problems originating in the 1980s and earlier. As you follow your course look out for articles on Lloyd's of London. Collect these so that you can appreciate how the Lloyd's market is developing.

Part 3

Case Studies

Business banking

Competition amongst the clearing banks to offer a modern range of products and appropriate service is severe. In recent years the banking industry has undergone extensive restructuring in order to remain well placed to serve business needs. Barclays Bank, and its business centre approach, is considered in this case study.

Barclays Business Centres

Meeting different requirements

As one of the major High Street banks, Barclays provides banking services to around 700,000 business customers ranging from sole traders to multinational corporations.

Appreciating that business customers have different and more complex requirements to that of personal customers, Barclays became the first bank to establish a network of specialist 'Business Centres' in 1987.

Centres of excellence

Business customers can obtain a wide range of advice and information on business banking at Barclays Business Centres nationwide.

In addition to the facilities and services currently available at any branch of Barclays, Business Centres can also provide their business customers with expertise and specialist services which until now have generally only been accessible in major commercial centres.

Understanding that business customers also have a requirement for personal banking services, the centres are also equipped to deal with personal customer needs. They are staffed by personal bankers, loans officers and counter staff who have been trained to accommodate a personal customer's banking requirements.

Fig 3.1 The Barclays Business Centre in Bromley
Source: Barclays Bank plc

Business banking teams

Business Centres are staffed by *business banking teams* comprising business bankers, small business managers, corporate managers and a Business Centre manager.

Business bankers look after business customers' everyday banking needs, small business managers service the needs of the small business customers, and corporate managers look after the requirements of middle market customers. The Business Centre manager will normally be responsible for the larger-sized businesses and oversee the overall business activity of the Business Centre.

All business banking teams have been specially trained to understand the needs of business customers and have the autonomy to make fast decisions when required. They appreciate that no two businesses are the same. Collectively, the teams have experience of dealing with businesses of all sizes and markets – from a sole trader to a multinational company.

Barclays believes that high calibre staff are fundamental to the success of its customers and to the bank itself. That is why considerable investment and emphasis is placed on staff training.

Location of Business Centres

There are specialist Business Centres strategically placed in most major towns, city centres and industrial estates throughout the UK.

Some business banking teams are based at sites which have been established away from the main local branch outlet – these sites are known as *management suites* and are accessible to business customers during regular working hours.

Business Centres have very good signposting within them, to enable business and personal customers to know where to go for assistance. Some Business Centres also have separate counter tills for their business customers.

Specialist facilities

Business Centres are useful for businesses which are already trading as well as those who are thinking of starting up.

Everyday business services such as insurance, pensions, short- and long-term finance and electronic payment facilities, can all be discussed with the business banking teams.

They can also provide businesses with access to specialists in particular fields such as agriculture, high technology, factoring and international trade. Businesses involved in importing and exporting, for example, can access information on local economies through Barclays Economic Departments and can locate buyers through its specialist Trade Development Service.

Where advice is required for non-banking issues, such as tax and legal problems, market research or training grants, business banking teams are able to signpost businesses to local specialists. Indeed, staff at Business Centres work very closely with other business support organisations like the Training and Enterprise Council (TEC), Enterprise Agency and the Chamber of Commerce, to ensure that a good network of advice and information is available to the local business community. In fact, Barclays, alongside these other business organisations, often runs joint seminars and workshops for businesses in the area.

Whatever requirements a business may have, Barclays Business Centres are well equipped to help them.

NIGEL PALMER – *Business Centre Manager*
JANE BAILEY – *Manager (Small Business Services)*

Commercial mortgage lending

Nationwide – 'the Nation's Building Society' – is well known for looking after personal customers – their Flex Account was highly innovative when launched in the eighties. However, their growing role in the business sector is probably less well appreciated. In this case study, David Brooker describes the way the Society serves the needs of its growing business customer base.

Nationwide Building Society

Nationwide's corporate vision is to become an outstanding successful provider of retail financial services by putting its members first with the offer of competitive products and quality service, treating everyone fairly and behaving as a responsible corporate citizen in its local community.

Nationwide Building Society is made up of a group of companies comprising the Building Society and its subsidiaries, some of which are Nationwide Trust, Nationwide Housing, Nationwide Estate Agents, all collectively known under the umbrella of Nationwide. The Society is the second largest in the UK with total assets of £35 billion and over 700 branches.

The Society's primary business is to raise funds and deposits through its retail network and from the major money markets via its Treasury Department in order to advance monies to individuals secured on residential property. In addition, Nationwide provides personal banking facilities, insurance products, unsecured loans and commercial mortgages. It also has, as previously mentioned, its own estate agency and one of the largest teams of surveyors in the UK.

In this study we will specifically be looking at Nationwide's commercial services which are handled through a department of the Society known as Special Financial Services. Special Financial Services handle the more complex lending cases. The areas covered are commercial mortgages, larger residential mortgages, bridging finance, negative equity and shortfalls. All cases are dealt with through relationship management with, on average, an account manager holding 150 active accounts.

Products

Here we are looking specifically at the commercial products. We are able to provide long-term mortgage loans for established businesses secured against freehold or long leasehold commercial property.

In general the length of loan is usually between five and twenty years with our borrowers being private limited companies, public companies, partnerships and sole traders. There is currently no restriction to lending in terms of amount; however, loan to value is restricted to a ratio of 70 per cent of the Society's own bricks and mortar valuation.

Repayment of loans may be by way of regular monthly capital and interest instalments, through interest only payments, in exceptional cases, covered by endowment or pensions with a final one-off payment to settle the loan. All loans are charged at either a margin over the Society's Mortgage Base Rate, three-month LIBOR rate or in terms of cash flow it may be more beneficial for borrowers to consider fixed rate mortgages which are available through the Society. Generally the repayment structure may be arranged to meet cash flow considerations.

Fees normally charged are at one per cent of the amount advanced and the Society would always take a first charge over the property involved as well as the assignment of any relevant endowment policies. In certain circumstances the Society may well also ask for fixed and floating charges for limited companies as well as personal guarantees from directors or other individuals and collateral security.

The Society in recent years has also developed deposit products aimed specifically at the commercial market through both off-shore funding in the Isle of Man and our business investor or treasury products. The Business Investor account is a business current account on which the Society pays interest on all deposits held and allows the businessman to make withdrawals by way of cheque (with restrictive features).

Adapting the products to suit customer business needs

When a business is making a property purchase for either its own occupation or investment purposes, it is important that it approaches the most appropriate source of funds to finance the transaction.

If the objective of the business is to own the property acquired for long-term occupation by either itself or tenants, one of the most appropriate sources of funds is a building society (Nationwide) with a commitment to assisting the business sector in addition to its traditional residential mortgage business. The business will be seeking to obtain a lending commitment from a well-established provider of financial services with the financial strength to support the lending over the period sought.

For the major capital outlay involved in property purchase long-term funding, maybe, is preferred as opposed to the shorter or medium term facilities associated with clearing banks. This gives the business peace of mind that it will not be called upon to repay the borrowing earlier than anticipated in the life of the property acquired.

It also assists the business with its forecasting and budgeting to have a stable pattern of repayments. If interest rates were to remain stable throughout the term of the funding then payments of capital and interest would be constant too. Whilst stable interest rates over the long term are an unlikely scenario, the risk of rising interest rates can be hedged through either fixed rates or through the purchase of an interest rate cap. (A cap ensures that interest rates cannot rise above a pre-determined maximum rate.) This would enhance the ability of the business to plan its cash flow for several years ahead.

The level of interest rates and associated costs charged in connection with funding of the property purchase will need to be at a competitive rate with up front costs at a level that are manageable bearing in mind the other costs involved in making a property purchase.

An example, therefore, could be where a company is currently renting its premises and paying a monthly rental of, say, £1,000 per month on a twenty-year lease with three-year rent reviews. The company is, therefore, aware that it is reasonably secure for the period of twenty years. However, at each three-year point it knows the likelihood is that its monthly payments will increase as the landlord demands more by way of rent. If, therefore, the company has an opportunity to purchase the freehold over a twenty-year period, it would assist the company potentially in the following ways:

1 It would have a freehold asset within the company's books strengthening the worth of the business.

2 It would also have the ability to fix its payments over a five-year or longer period and would more than likely be making monthly payments of less than that expected through the normal rent.

3 It would also have the ability in owning its own freehold to potentially borrow further sums against it whereas if it stayed within the leasehold arrangement it would have no additional security to bargain with for further funding, say perhaps from its bankers.

One can, therefore, immediately see that there are advantages in a company owning its own freehold premises. The same could also apply in terms of individuals looking to build an investment portfolio. It should, however, be borne in mind that the Society only has the ability to lend on term loans, it does not have the ability commercially to provide overdraft facilities.

The conclusion is that businesses need professional one-to-one relationships with a lender which can be provided by a designated Account Manager, such as that provided by the Nationwide, who is able to offer advice together with other products and services designed to fit the business needs. Nationwide's Special Financial Services, with its team of locally based Account Managers, is ideally placed to meet the individual needs of business with a quality service.

DAVID BROOKER ACIB MCIM
Area Support Manager, Nationwide Building Society, Special Financial Services

Corporate banking in a retail bank

Every bank has its own unique method of grouping corporate customers and also has its own culture; that is to say that each separate bank has its own way of doing things. Whilst it is true that the major retail banks all offer broadly similar products to the very large multinational corporates which operate in the UK, in this study Anastasia Micklethwaite describes her own views of the Corporate Banking Division of Lloyds Bank Plc.

The business of corporate banking

Corporate banking covers a multitude of activities. The maintenance of the customer/bank relationship is arguably the most important aspect as this is how contacts are built up and rapport is established. It is also in this respect that many corporates perceive service quality – an important factor, especially when companies are putting their banking out to tender. Many banks divide their staff into small specialised teams where managers and their assistants are responsible for a particular group of customers, usually defined by industry sector. The type of work on each team will vary greatly as the nature of banking services which particular sectors require also varies. Some sectors such as retail stores and supermarkets require heavy money transmission services in order to process all their cash and cheques, whilst other sectors such as the heavy transport industries or manufacturers have less of a need for money transmission business, but require very specific loan packages and guarantees which need to be tailored to their requirements.

Corporate banking is not just simply about cheque processing and the lending of money. It encompasses a whole range of products and services and the use of information technology continues to play a more important role in banking as time progresses. Electronic banking now enables customers to make payments from computer terminals or call up balances without even leaving their offices. Other systems enable the treasury departments of banks to buy and sell foreign currency for their corporate customers whilst stockbrokers can now facilitate the buying and selling of company debt and equity at the touch of a screen.

Another important role of a corporate banking Treasury Department is to facilitate the 'swapping' of fixed interest rates for floating interest rates (and vice versa) for major corporate customers, thus enabling each party to find a rate which is suitable for their purposes. Treasury is also responsible for taking in money market deposits for specified periods and for dealing on the market.

A Trade and Project Finance Division may exist within corporate banking in order to negotiate and arrange large-scale project lending or to set up banking facilities for specific trading. Examples would include the financing of a major international project for a particular customer or giving a guarantee to a third party that the bank's customer will pay on delivery for large shipments of goods.

Capital Market Divisions exist under the banner of Corporate Banking to facilitate bond dealing or the purchase and resale of debt for commercial paper.

A Leasing Division often operates within Corporate Banking. This enables companies to lease out costly equipment at a set fee at regular intervals, thereby enabling corporate customers to make use of equipment that they would otherwise have been unable to afford and purchase outright. A typical example is the leasing of commercial

Fig 3.2 Manufacturers such as BAe may need a range of products from their bankers involving complex currency, money transfer and funding issues
Source: British Aerospace

airliners. Many planes are actually owned by large banks and leased out to companies for a specific fee and at a set rate over a period of time.

The relationship manager

The responsibilities of those on the corporate banking teams can be very wide ranging and cover such diverse activities as liaising between branches and company finance departments in order to resolve money transmission queries or putting forward recommendations for loan deals worth millions of pounds. A sound knowledge of branch procedures and money transmission products is required and numeracy is an asset as the comprehension of balance sheets and statistics becomes increasingly important.

The ability to quickly establish rapport with a wide range of people is a prerequisite as discussions take place which can involve bank branches and company administrators and also between the most senior members of the bank and finance directors and/or treasurers of major international companies.

Staff are recruited to corporate banking either internally through other areas of the bank or by direct recruitment on leaving university. All staff are trained not only in the department, but in branches, due to the importance of the understanding of branch procedures in day-to-day work. Graduate recruitment continues year on year, although the recruitment of school leavers at GCSE level has slowed down to negligible levels in recent years. Some banks have not recruited from schools at all in the past three years.

Categorising corporate customers

Corporate banking customers are more often than not defined by turnover, that is, the amount of sales revenue that is taken in to the group or company on an annual basis. Many retail banks provide for small business customers such as local shops or small firms through a local branch or a small business centre. Small businesses could roughly be defined as those with a turnover of a million pounds or below each year.

Those customers which we so often describe as 'medium sized corporates' with turnover of between £1 million and £50 million are usually provided for by specialised commercial banking staff in regional offices. The physical processing of the company's cheques and the maintenance of their actual bank accounts are still done at branch level, but the contact persons who are responsible for the actual bank/customer relationships and who have the specialised knowledge and expertise, are based around the country in regional centres such as those in London, Manchester and Leeds.

The prime corporate customers of the major retail banks are more often than not, very large, often multinational groups whose turnover may vary from around £50 million to billions of pounds. Alternatively they can be grouped by *tangible net worth*. This is the total amount of capital invested in the business plus any reserved profits. Large corporates would have a net worth of anything from £25 million upwards. The groups themselves may encompass several subsidiary companies and their banking may well be divided between two or more major banks. The retail banks generally have a separate Corporate Banking Division, usually based in London, where specialised teams perform the 'Relationship Banking' role described above for these important customers. Again, the physical processing of cheques and cash (money transmission) is carried out within the branch network or in external processing sites around the country. Some banks have set up specialised branches or processing centres to handle only large corporate business, thereby pooling expert staff who are familiar with the running of very large business accounts.

Some of the larger corporations choose to divide their banking business, and it is not uncommon for some subsidiaries of a particular group to have their money transmission business with one bank and for the other subsidiaries to have their banking with another. Corporate lending and project finance may be divided amongst several banks all offering different products, or alternatively these same institutions may share the lending of a specific facility to a group.

ANASTASIA MICKLETHWAITE MA (Cantab.) ARCM
Assistant Manager, Corporate Banking Division, Lloyds Bank Plc

Factoring – a modern solution

The factoring industry offers business a unique solution to its needs for finance: a borrowing facility which, by being linked to sales turnover, actually grows with the business. Through the employment of the most modern technology funds can be available within twenty-four hours. Russell Marlow describes how Griffin Factors provides this facility.

GRIFFIN FACTORS
Cashflow for Business

As a Relationship Manager for Griffin Factors Limited, I am responsible for a portfolio of corporate clients who between them are advanced approximately £25 million by my company at any one time and turn over in excess of £300 million per annum. My job involves managing risk, providing excellent client service and cross-selling additional Griffin services. The contribution made by our small team towards Griffin's overall success is significant and highly rewarding.

Griffin Factors Ltd is a wholly owned subsidiary of Midland Bank, itself part of the strong international banking group Hong Kong and Shanghai Banking Corporation. Griffin has the distinction of being the UK's most profitable factoring company for the last six years, and has achieved year-on-year growth for the last ten years.

Factoring is still only thirty years old in the UK and the industry remains highly focused, offering clearly defined and specialist services. Griffin provides three basic services:

- sales-linked funding
- credit protection
- sales ledger management

It delivers these services through the following products:

- Disclosed factoring (sales ledger management, funding and optional credit protection)

- Confidential invoice discounting (funding and optional credit protection)
- Export factoring (cross border sales ledger management, funding and credit protection)

The common and most important feature is the availability of funding relating to current trading activity, normally at the rate of 80 per cent of 'good' trade credit invoices. The 80 per cent 'prepayment' made at the time an invoice is raised allows the client to meet its working capital commitments and in most cases gives the business access to a far higher working capital facility than would be available from a bank.

It is well known that growing companies, or those rebuilding after

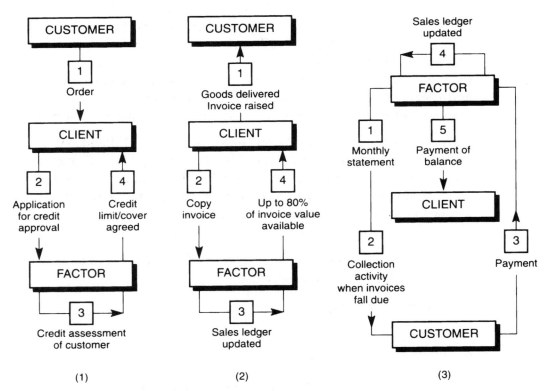

Fig 3.3 How factoring works
(1) Application for credit
(2) Delivery of goods and invoice raised
(3) Payment and collection
Source: Griffin Factors

recession, have a high requirement for cash. Yet a bank will look at yesterday's balance sheet for comfort, and will find little in either case to support current requirements. A bank will worry if its corporate customer constantly seeks to increase its overdraft facility to fund increasing sales for fear that the business is overtrading.

Factoring is not a solution to overtrading, but it removes the risks of overtrading in all but the most extreme cases. By analysing current customers and monitoring the value of a client's sales ledger closely, a factor can provide a facility that is relevant to current activity and which grows automatically in line with increasing sales. Griffin has made it possible for its clients to achieve significant increases in sales, thereby spreading overheads and reaching the high ground of sustained profitability. Ultimately this may lead to a public flotation, repayment of all debts through retained profits, or allow existing shareholders to sell the business at significant personal profit in order to retire.

However, not all businesses or invoices can be funded by a factor. A factor is able to provide generous facilities because it does not lose sight of a key principle – each debt funded must be collectable, even if the worst happened and the client failed. This requirement excludes a number of scenarios.

- Whole industries are not 'factorable'. This would include building (outstanding debts would not be paid if jobs are not completed), works subject to contract or stage payments, e.g. capital projects, computer software development or advertising, all of which can be subject to dispute. In simple terms, factors like clients with products that meet the description 'buy, sell and forget' where the resultant debt is easily proven and payable in isolation to any other matters. It is a matter of judgement what products and services meet this criteria. Where a client's business is factorable, the factor then assesses the sales ledger itself. Griffin will look to match its funding against the value of the underlying debts.

- Funding is, therefore, not provided against debts that are substantially overdue for payment, disputed debts, 'concentration' debtors and debtor credit limit excesses.

A concentration of the client's business with one customer presents a strategic risk to the client and is discouraged. Funding is restricted on any one debtor to 30 per cent of the total sales ledger, to encourage a good spread of risk, for client and factor. If this policy were not pursued, a debtor bad debt could easily turn into a client bad debt for the factor.

Debtor credit limits are particularly important to Griffin which undertakes specific debtor assessment, unlike many factors which do not offer this service. Limits are set on individual debtor accounts, above which funding (or credit protection) is not available. This not only limits the factor's exposure to prudent levels or uncreditworthy debtors, but provides the clients with invaluable guidelines to help them improve the quality of their customer base.

Whilst the factor is theoretically well secured by having title to the book debts by way of assignment (often supplemented by a fixed charge), relationship and credit and risk management is far from relaxed. More often than not, Griffin is the principal funder to its clients and the clearing bank adopts a very low profile. Based in Worthing on the south coast, I control an invoice discounting portfolio of clients in the north west of England. The distance demands maximum utilisation of time to benefit both Griffin and the client. Many clients look to the factor to replace the bank not only for cash but as their main 'sounding board'.

Through the quality of its relationship managers, Griffin adds value to the basic services, helping to remove what has become the dated and adverse perception of factoring. Modern businessmen are pragmatic and expect high quality and good value from their suppliers and it is the job of the relationship manager to ensure that clients continue to buy into those concepts from Griffin and that Griffin continues to meet the underlying needs of the business.

The Griffin relationship manager needs to be a sharp judge of character, an astute financial analyst, a good negotiator and professional in order to command respect. Avoidance of fraud is now a key challenge, whilst developing business partnership and relationship skills begin to dominate the agenda. The opportunity to travel, meet business people and see different types of business from timber merchant to car exhaust manufacturer, haulier to heavy engineer, UPVC window manufacturer to printer, provides ample motivation to high achieving individuals.

Funding book debt demands a knowledge of the mechanics of each industry and for me this has meant broadening horizons not only regarding a number of industries but allowing an insight into the way enterprise flourishes in different parts of the country.

Factoring is built upon a fairly weak legal foundation where case law and practice contributes to the legal framework. The industry body, the Association of British Factors and Discounters (ABF&D) runs Certificate and Diploma courses for member companies, which allow staff to become highly qualified at a level comparable to banking and accountancy. Having completed both courses, the job becomes far more rewarding.

Fig 3.4 Well-known companies like Eddie Stobart Ltd have grown with the help of invoice discounting
Source: Eddie Stobart Ltd

A final word on the future. Factoring has grown very quickly and is now a highly competitive market. Factors have taken a large share of traditional bank overdraft lending and there will need to be an increase in sophistication and flexibility in order to consolidate and develop that position. Increasing emphasis on service levels and quality will require clever systems and highly trained personnel. The trend towards Electronic Data Interchange (EDI) will revolutionise the factoring operation and will require investment in systems. New products and enhancement of existing ones, client retention strategies and new business growth will dominate the push forward.

Griffin takes all of these and other challenges on board. It is an exciting, enthusiastic and energetic environment in which to work and I hope this study has provided a useful insight into my company and its products, people and clients.

RUSSELL MARLOW DipFS ACIB AIL
Relationship Manager, Griffin Factors Limited

London International Financial Futures and Options Exchange

The London International Financial Futures and Options Exchange (LIFFE) is a modern market, but though it incorporates new technology there is somehow a very traditional feel to it. The combination of open outcry, unique products, confusing jargon and computers in modern premises may seem bewildering to many. Maxine Wood first encountered all this through a work experience placement, whilst undertaking a college course, where Financial Services was her first choice option.

LIFFE

When I wrote this I was a student at Bromley College of Further and Higher Education, studying for a BTEC National Diploma in Business and Finance. During my second year I was lucky enough to gain a two-week work experience placement as a runner in the futures market. The market's formal name is The London International Financial Futures and Options Exchange.

The first thing I noticed about the market was its size; it contains twenty-one 'pits' spread out across the trading floor (one for each 'contract'), and these cover a considerable area. The second thing I noticed was the noise; it can be deafening. The LIFFE market is one of the last markets in England to use 'open outcry' trading, as opposed to the increasingly more common conventional computer trading.

LIFFE provides risk management and trading opportunities in fixed income, treasury and equity products. They are denominated in contracts of German Marks, US Dollars, Sterling, Japanese Yen, Swiss Francs, European Currency Units (ECU) and Italian Lire.

LIFFE works by providing financial futures and options contracts.

What are futures and options?

Futures and options are contracts – that is, legally binding agreements – to buy or sell something in the future. That 'something' could be a contract to secure an interest rate or a company share price for example. Each contract specifies the quantity of the item, and also the time of delivery or payment.

The buyer and seller of a futures contract agree on a price today for a product to be delivered and paid for in the future. The buyer of an option purchases the right – but not the obligation – to buy or sell a futures contract, or a company share, at a particular price on a certain date in the future. The seller of an option will be obliged to buy or to sell if the buyer decides to exercise his option.

Futures and options based on a wide variety of financial instruments are traded at LIFFE.

Source: LIFFE

As an example consider the case of a company which feels that, due to a deal it is hoping to secure, it may need to borrow a significant amount of money, in eight months time. It turns to the LIFFE market and purchases an option as a form of 'insurance'. By purchasing an option it can lock itself into a maximum interest rate for the borrowing requirement. If real interest rates decline it can secure funding in the normal way at a lower cost. If it later finds it has no need to borrow then the option can be sold or exercised for its market value (if any), and the only loss will have been their original cost (i.e. premium).

The staff of member companies of LIFFE all wear brightly coloured jackets, along with an identity badge bearing their full name and company's mnemonic, which provides instant ease of identification. Bright red or multicoloured jackets are worn by qualified traders. Blue jackets are worn by LIFFE officials and pit observers, who are there in a supervisory role and not to trade. Pit observers ensure that trading is conducted according to the rules. They monitor prices that are traded, and they relay price information which is keyed into computer terminals. New prices appear immediately on LIFFE's in-house computer system, and are then transmitted worldwide.

Yellow jackets are worn by the administrative staff of each member company. Most of them are also training to become traders. All traders will have been a yellow jacket for at least six months, and will have passed LIFFE's floor trader's course and examinations.

To understand how a deal is executed I will guide you through the basic information that appears on a computer terminal used by a trading company (see Figure 3.5).

Order number	provides ease of access if there are any problems with a trade. Every trade has a different order number.
T B F	T stands for trade; the space in the middle is either a B (Bought) or S (Sold). The F stands for Future.
Home trader	Each trader has his own mnemonic; no two traders can have the same mnemonic.

Contract month	The contract in this case is G; this stands for gilts. Z in the example is the month (December).
Counterparty dealer	The mnemonic of the dealer from the other company.
Price and quantity	As agreed between the two traders in the pit.
Counterparty company	The company for which dealer DEF is working.
Slip number	The confirmation slip number, which is written out and given to company XYZ to match their trade.

Fig 3.5 Trading details

This data actually appears on one half of the computer screen; the other side will be filled when the other company – in this case XYZ – have tapped their side of the information into their computer. If both match, the other side of the screen will be considered complete. If, however, the deal has not matched exactly, a U will appear next to the time column, to show that the trade is unmatched. At this point a runner ('Yellow Jacket') has to go to the other company's booth to disagree the trade. There are a whole host of reasons why a trade doesn't match, such as the wrong price, the wrong company, the wrong dealer. If, after double checking the dealer cards and computer screens of both companies, there is still an anomaly, the matter has to be taken to the traders in the pit who traded that deal. If after this stage no agreement can be made, both parties have to watch a video playback of the deal (as cameras record every trade in the pit), and only then can a final decision be made.

How LIFFE works - the route of a LIFFE trade

- A client wishes to buy or sell futures or options and telephones his broker.

- The broker contacts a LIFFE member booth on the LIFFE trading floor with his client's instructions. The order is received in the booth and time stamped.

- The pit trader is given the information either by hand signals or by written order from the booth clerk. It is then offered to other traders in the pit.

- The trader who responds to the offer becomes the counterparty to the deal.

- The broker then informs his client that his order is filled.

- Both parties complete a clearing slip which is entered into LIFFE's Trade Registration System (TRS), or alternatively, the information is keyed directly into TRS.

- Confirmed trades are then passed to the London Clearing House (LCH), for clearing. The LCH acts as the counterparty to all clearing members for all registered positions. LCH collects and pays margins to clearing members who in turn collect margins from clients.

I found my work experience placement highly rewarding as I learned about the LIFFE market and specifically the kind of job opportunities available. One week after the placement finished I switched from the full-time course at college to a job at LIFFE, and I now aim to secure a BTEC National qualification through evening classes.

MAXINE WOOD

MONDEX – the alternative to cash

Cash still dominates the global payments market – in fact cash accounts for approximately 90 per cent of all transactions. Alternative payment mechanisms, including credit cards, capture just 10 per cent. In this case study Leane Fontana considers Mondex, an exciting alternative to cash. Leane produced this study as a final assignment on her BTEC course and was guided by Neil Evans of the Midland Bank. She was grateful for the support of the Mondex units of both the Midland Bank and the National Westminster Bank.

What is Mondex?

'Mondex', the new electronic alternative to cash, is based on smart card technology, and was only invented in 1990. Mondex is actually a system for delivering and receiving cash electronically via a highly sophisticated smart card. Whilst Mondex is not initially anticipated to completely replace cash, it is seen as a highly adaptable substitute for it.

Tim Jones, the creator, believes that Mondex will provide an invaluable alternative to cash in your purse or pocket, funds in a retailer's till and balances in a bank account because it has additional features that could revolutionise the whole concept of money.

NatWest are to create a new company called MONDEX International. This will then market Mondex to leading banks around the globe. The concept will be sold as a franchise with the first, in the UK, to be operated by Midland and NatWest with support from British Telecom.

How Mondex works

Initially a Mondex user will load the card with funds from a bank account using specifically adapted ATMs or by using Mondex-compatible BT telephones. Retailers receive payment from a customer's card for goods sold and will typically, at the end of the day, send their 'cash balances' down the telephone line to their bank accounts.

Fig 3.6 Mondex – electronic cash
Source: Mondex UK Ltd

Mondex utilises what could best be described as an 'electronic wallet'. This is a device which resembles an electronic calculator, into which the cardholders can slot their cards. A cardholder might then call up details of the last ten transactions and check their balance. The card can be 'locked' and 'unlocked' electronically using a personal code number. The wallet, which can load and unload value from other Mondex cards, will allow one cardholder to transfer funds to another. The wallet also acts as a terminal for small scale retailers and street traders.

The scheme will ultimately be controlled by a purse operator, which will guarantee the value of transactions at every point in the system and will, furthermore, provide a clearing and settlement service.

Mondex will therefore work as follows:

1 A Mondex smart card will be issued by the purse operator.

2 This card will be loaded with electronic money through a

withdrawal from a bank account using an ATM or compatible telephone. The card-user will decide how much money to put on the card with an awareness of what is available in their bank account, and what expenditure they anticipate making.

3 The electronic money on the card is then used as payment for goods and services: funds are transferred from the card to the retailer's terminal or to other cardholders via a wallet.

4 Retailers transfer Mondex Cash collected from cardholders directly to their business bank account using a Mondex-compatible telephone or ATM.

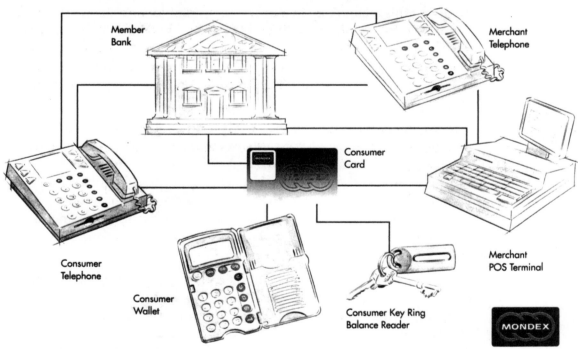

Fig 3.7 Mondex payments scheme

Source: Mondex UK Ltd

New technology

Each Mondex card utilises a small silicon chip. The chip will receive, store and transfer value to a similar chip in the recipient's own Mondex card.

Transactions will be conditional upon the following:

- the payer having adequate value stored in their card to cover the payment, and
- one card releasing value and the other accepting it, each confirming the authenticity of the other.

Each time funds are exchanged, the chips involved check that there has been no tampering with the transactions en route. Purse number one will question purse number two: 'I am a Mondex member, are you?' Only if they both 'check out' will they exchange value.

By using this technology in a universal format around the world even cards held by people from different countries will be able to undertake transactions, provided they are in the same currency. As cards will be able to carry up to five currencies, a business traveller from the UK might typically hold some US dollars, or Deutschmarks on their card all the time.

The testing of MONDEX began in Swindon in July 1995. I anticipate it will become a key product for retailers and consumers over the next few years.

THE MONDEX OPPORTUNITY

The market for cash payments and therefore the opportunity for Mondex is immense.

Mondex has been designed as a true cash alternative replicating the core features of cash but providing new degrees of convenience, flexibility, security and control. Mondex provides the opportunity to:

- Carry electronic cash in a clean and convenient plastic card
- Obtain electronic cash readily and from the comfort of home
- Make immediate and exact payments without the need to count out change
- Check a record of previous transactions
- Carry up to five different currencies on one card
- Send electronic cash anywhere in the world.

Market research has identified consumer enthusiasm for Mondex as an addition to the existing range of payment options. For merchants too, Mondex provides a simple, efficient and secure alternative to traditional notes and coins.

Mondex offers the potential for a new global payment scheme within which:

- Mondex cards are readily available from banks, financial institutions and other organisations
- Mondex cardholders are able to get access to their money almost anywhere, at any time: at cash machines, public payphones, in the office and at home
- Merchants of any size, around the world, accept Mondex readily
- Electronic cash circulates freely between consumers, banks and businesses just as notes and coins do now
- Mondex devices, offering a host of added value applications, are produced by manufacturers all over the world.

Mondex offers the potential to become the worldwide alternative to cash.

Source: National Westminster Bank Plc

THE BENEFITS FOR MERCHANTS

The benefits for merchants have been tested in a major research study involving 35 leading US retail and public service corporations and 16 smaller single or multi unit retailers. The following benefits were identified:

Greater efficiency at the point of sale
- Customer identification, signature or PIN entry is not required
- Payment authorisation is not necessary
- Mondex payments are exact – there is no need to give change
- Mondex payments take less than three seconds to complete.

Low start up cost
- The only hardware a merchant requires is an inexpensive Mondex Terminal – no new telephone lines or computer facilities. Minimal staff training is required to operate the system.

More flexibility
- Because Mondex payments are fast and cheap they are suitable for all types of merchant and any size of payment
- The pocket sized Mondex Wallet can be used as an inexpensive and compact point of sale terminal suitable in environments where a Retailer Terminal is not appropriate – market stalls and taxis for example.

Marketing opportunity
- Mondex will allow merchants to capitalise on the opportunity offered by smart cards to run customer loyalty schemes. If customers choose to join a loyalty scheme, a merchant can automatically record each use of their cards. With such detailed information, merchants can offer sophisticated discounts and special offers to reward their loyal customers.

Extra security, lower costs
- Mondex value held in merchant terminals can be electronically locked reducing both the cost and security risks associated with storing, counting and transporting physical notes and coins
- Mondex takings can be banked at any time through the telephone network.

Source: National Westminster Bank Plc

Pension and investment advice

Abbey National, once the United Kingdom's second largest building society, and now a bank, has a well-established presence and brand name in the financial services sector. A strategic decision to use this market standing and develop a subsidiary to advise on pensions and other investment opportunities, led to the creation of Abbey National Financial Services Ltd. Wendy Breen and her colleagues reveal what this company can offer to a business.

Abbey National Financial Services Limited is a wholly owned subsidiary of Abbey National plc. The company was formed during the latter months of 1987 and commenced trading on 2 January 1988. Following the enactment of the Financial Services Act 1986 the concept of *polarisation* became a requirement. Polarisation means that every firm (including sole traders) which advises on or arranges investments has a fundamental choice:

Either seek authorisation themselves as an **independent intermediary** with the ability to recommend investments from all providers, or become the appointed representative of ('tie to') an authorised firm.

Abbey National plc chose to become an appointed representative of Friends Provident Life Office. This arrangement was modified with the formation, in 1993, of Abbey National Life. Abbey National plc is now an appointed representative of that company. At the same time that the decision was made to tie to Friends Provident it was decided to form Abbey National Financial Services Limited as an independent intermediary. Under the requirements of the Financial Services Act 1986 Abbey National Financial Services Limited is authorised in the conduct of investment business by the Securities and Investments Board.

The company maintains nine area sales offices located in:

Birmingham	Sevenoaks
Bristol	Sheffield
Chelmsford	Wigan
Glasgow	Woking
High Wycombe	

The nine offices between them support in excess of 320 financial planning consultants. The revenue generated by these consultants places the company among the top ten independent financial advisers in the United Kingdom. Although some referrals are made by Abbey National plc, more than 95 per cent of Abbey National Financial Services Limited's revenue income is generated via the nine area sales offices.

Abbey National Financial Services Limited sees its main market as being among those members of the public and corporate bodies who appreciate the advantages of independent financial advice.

HOW WE LOOK AFTER YOUR INTERESTS

Our double reassurance of security
As an Independent Intermediary authorised by the Securities and Investments Board, we are bound by its rules under the Financial Services Act. This means that we are not tied to any insurance company but are, instead, able to survey the entire market to give you unbiased advice on the products most suitable to you.

This reassurance of security is doubled by the fact that, as a wholly owned subsidiary of Abbey National plc, we operate with the same high standards of integrity.

What we can do for you
Because we are an Independent Intermediary, our Financial Planning Consultants are authorised to advise on life insurance policies, pension contracts, personal equity plans and authorised unit trust schemes. Most products we recommend are of a long-term nature and early cancellation could have an adverse effect on your investment. You have a right to change your mind before you finally commit yourself to buying the product recommended by us. If you do change your mind, please contact us as soon as possible. It could be we have not fully explained the nature of the product. We do not accept discretionary authority to manage our clients' investments: each transaction will require your specific authority. If you do want help in this area, we can refer you to another Independent Intermediary. Naturally, if we receive any commission from this adviser, we will inform you.

Source: Terms of Business and Company Policy

Key services

Abbey National Financial Services Limited is able to offer a wide range of personal and corporate financial planning advice including:

1 'Global' personal financial planning covering all aspects of:

- Dependent protection
- Retirement planning
- Regular savings
- Capital investment
- Estate and tax planning.

2 Corporate Financial Planning including:

- Partnership protection
- Directors' share purchase protection
- Key person insurance
- Corporate financing
- Occupational pension planning
- Corporate investment
- Corporate tax planning.

In addition to the above Abbey National Financial Services Limited is able to offer the public and corporate bodies alike seminars on:

- Investment and taxation
- Mid-life financial planning
- Redundancy counselling
- Retirement planning.

Also available are the services of the Abbey National Financial Services Limited Employee Benefits Division who are able to offer additional corporate services such as:

- The installation of share-save schemes
- Group sickness and accident schemes
- Group medical insurance schemes.

All business activities of the staff of Abbey National Financial Services Limited must be conducted with an awareness of the company's obligations under the Financial Services Act. All members of the companies who offer advice on investment products are trained and examined in the requirements of the Act.

The policy of Abbey National Financial Services Limited is to get to know the client, assessing their individual situation and taking into account their needs, hopes for the future and financial priorities. Then the company will research the market and recommend a plan designed to meet their needs and achieve their financial objectives.

The company's aim is always to give best advice.

WENDY BREEN, *Financial Planning Consultant*
and
GRAHAM LOWE, *Sales Director*
RON LELLOW, *Product Training Manager*
JEFF HUTCHINSON, *Sales Development Consultant*
MICHAEL BEER, *Marketing Manager*
GILLIAN SALT, *Compliance Manager*

Abbey National Financial Services Limited

Protecting both assets and individuals

Eagle Star, which is wholly owned by B.A.T. Industries, is one of the UK's largest life and general insurers. In this study they explain their structure and market standing. Furthermore, they review some of the key products which they offer to a range of individuals and businesses which constitute the corporate sector.

EAGLE STAR

Eagle Star is one of the UK's leading life and general insurers and non-life reinsurers. It is a leader in motor, household, travel, yacht and employers' liability insurance, and a major supplier of life assurance, pensions and investment products.

The company employs around 13,500 people worldwide and markets a wide range of general and life products in some thirty countries across Europe, the Middle East, Asia and Latin America.

Funds under management amounted to £14 billion in 1994 with general and life net premium income totalling £2,990 million.

Corporate structure

Eagle Star is wholly owned by B.A.T. Industries, one of the UK's largest business enterprises and a leading provider of personal financial and insurance services in the UK and North America. It is the 6th largest composite insurer in the UK and 4th largest general insurer. It is in the top 25 for life pensions and unit trusts.

In UK financial services, B.A.T. is the largest UK-based insurance group, owning also Allied Dunbar, Britain's leading unit-linked life assurance and pensions company, and Threadneedle Asset Management, one of the UK's largest institutional investors.

History

- Eagle Star's origins date back to the Eagle Company, founded in 1807, and the Star Company of 1843.

- British Dominions Marine Insurance Company, established by Sir Edward Mountain in the early 1900s, took over the Eagle and the Star in 1917, thereby creating one of Britain's first composite insurers. The title Eagle Star was adopted in 1937.

- Eagle Star became part of B.A.T. Industries in 1984 and it was its first acquisition as part of its policy of diversifying into financial services.

Eagle Star commercial insurance

Eagle Star is one of the leading commercial lines insurers in the UK, with £594 million of commercial net premium income in 1994. It is the market leader in employers' liability insurance, and is the largest commercial motor/fleet insurer in Britain.

It is in the top six for commercial property insurance, and is a leading provider of risk management services to UK industry through its Engineering Consultancy Services arm and engineering insurance.

Key products and features

Tradestar range

- Packaged policies encompassing a wide range of cover for small- to medium-sized businesses.

- Specialist versions include Tradestar Shop, Office, Business.

Commercial Motor

- Policies for office, business, commercial cars and goods carrying vehicles.

- Associated risk management service including management information system for fleet managers, providing details of accident/theft rates and claims record.

Commercial Property

- Cover for commercial properties, including offices, factories, schools/universities and government buildings.
- Non-collateral damage from fire covered by Business Interruption policy.
- Professional risk surveys provide guidance on loss control.

Combined Policy

- Flexibility to select from a range of key covers that are fundamental to the small- and medium-sized business – the most essential commercial insurances in one policy.

Engineering

- Specialist policies for plant, contractors' equipment, construction sites.
- Consultancy Services provide expert risk management advice and guidance on health and safety at work for employers in the manufacturing and service sectors.

Pluvius

- Insurance for specific outdoor events, e.g. weddings, fêtes, sports events and flower shows against unfavourable weather or lack of rain or snow.

Eagle Star Life

Eagle Star is a major provider of life insurance, pensions, investments and protection in the UK and selected markets overseas. Its policies are sold direct and through independent financial advisers, appointed representatives and major financial institutions like the Bristol and West Building Society.

New worldwide weighted premiums and unit trust sales (annual premiums plus 10 per cent of new single premiums) were £152m in 1994.

In the UK, Eagle Star Life is especially strong in care and protection products (including nursing and residential home fees plans), pensions (individual and group), unit trusts and PEPs, and mortgage-related policies.

Key products

Care and protection

- Term Assurance
- Flexible Whole Life Assurance
- Critical Illness
- Permanent Health Insurance
- Care Fees Payment Plan

Savings and investments

- Guaranteed Investment Bonds
- Unit Trusts
- PEPs
- Unit-linked savings plans

Mortgage-related

- Endowment mortgages
- PEP and pension mortgages
- Decreasing term assurance (mortgage protection)

Pensions

- Individual and Group Personal Pensions – The Personal Pension Account is a flexible plan designed to take maximum advantage of the favourable tax treatment of pensions coupled with the potential for excellent investment growth. The account is appropriate for both the self-employed and those in non-pensionable occupations. A group arrangement is available for a minimum of five lives. Enhanced terms are available.

- Free Standing AVCs – The AVC Plan is designed to top up the benefits of an employer's scheme combining all the tax advantages of pensions with the potential for excellent investment growth. The plan is particularly relevant for those who have changed jobs or who wish to retire early.

- Executive Pension Plans – This plan is open to any company director or an employee with Schedule E earnings. The arrangement is designed to be 'exempt approved' under Chapter 1 of Part XIV of the Income and Corporation Taxes Act 1988. The benefits provided on retirement or death for each member under the plan are secured by the policy of assurance taken out by the trustees of the plan. Additionally, there are two investment only policies available, namely Trustee Investment Plan (TIP) and Trustee Executive Plan (TEP). We also offer a Small Self Administered Scheme (SSAS).

Eagle Star Re

Eagle Star Re is the UK's largest non-life reinsurance company, with share capital of £175m. It was created in 1993 from the long-established marine and reinsurance and London Market operations of Eagle Star.

It is active in most of the world's major non-marine and marine markets, and provides support for local insurance companies, for shipowners and for trading concerns in more than one hundred countries. It underwrites in the UK and has branches in Tokyo, Rotterdam and Amsterdam.

Fund management

In May 1994, the decision was made to merge the fund management activities of Eagle Star with those of Allied Dunbar, to form a new company – Threadneedle Asset Management. Based in London and Swindon, Threadneedle employs some 280 staff and manages approaching £30 billion of funds and is one of the top institutional investors in the UK.

Eagle Star is based in Cheltenham, Gloucestershire and has offices in the City of London and throughout the UK. The company also trades in over thirty countries worldwide.

Small business insurance

In the increasingly difficult and competitive commercial environment a business needs to protect itself against a multitude of risks. This is a complex area and deserves the attention of the business manager. Detailed research is needed and sound advice should always be sought. Julian Childs, who advises businesses through his Bromley based firm, Mainly Marketing, considers the key issues in this case study.

Insuring your business

When you are just starting up in business and every penny is critical, paying insurance premiums can seem to be an uncalled-for imposition. Deciding what insurance you should have must rate as one of the least exciting decisions you have to make for your business. Paying out money to cover you against hazards which you fervently hope will not happen, ranks fairly low in satisfaction.

But you would see this in a different light if the occasion arose to put in a claim – then you might worry about whether you had taken enough insurance to cover all the losses you had suffered. After all, failing to get the right insurance might mean the collapse and end of your business.

Insurance is best thought of as the price of 'peace of mind' – accidents can and do happen. But make sure, if you take out insurance, that the cover is adequate – otherwise you might as well not bother. Almost every aspect of trading can create a need for some kind of insurance. For most kinds you can find cover, but sometimes the premium may be high.

Although the premiums paid for any business insurance are deductible expenses which can be set off against tax, it is essential to look at insurance from the start of your business planning and build realistic premiums into your cash flow forecasts – they may change all your assumptions on profitability and the time to discover that is now, and not when you are already committed financially.

As I have suggested, insurance can be complicated so let us consider the issues as follows:

- Choosing and buying insurance for business
- Insurance required by law and contract
- Essential insurance
- Highly desirable insurance
- 'When you can afford it' insurance

Choosing and buying insurance for business

Dealing with the public for money is business: it does not matter whether it is a multi-billion corporation or a weekend job repairing lawnmowers. The business that needs no additional insurance is a comparative rarity. You should be aware that business use affects your usual household insurance. You may be sued by a customer who enters your premises and suffers an accident; your household 'public liability' cover is not appropriate. Equipment such as computers which are used at home for work purposes do not count as part of the household goods for fire and theft purposes. And of course you must make sure you have adequate insurance for your car.

In any case and in many ways businesses are just like people: they operate under the same risks and face the same perils. Their assets can be lost, stolen or damaged; the death of a partner, an owner or a key member of staff can have the same financial effect on a company as the death of the breadwinner in a family. Unlike people, however, businesses need not die, as long as proper precautions are taken against the risks. Anyone running a small business therefore needs to look carefully at insurance to ensure the current running and future prospects of the business, but arranging appropriate cover to meet the needs of an individual business can be a complicated, time-consuming and costly exercise. Because of advertising, and perhaps previous experience, you will already know of many of the big insurance companies handling commercial or business insurances – e.g. Eagle Star, Commercial Union, Royal, Guardian Royal Exchange, General Accident, Sun Alliance, Zurich, Norwich Union etc. Another name much in the news, but which nevertheless has an excellent reputation for expertise, flexibility, cost-effectiveness and claims settlement is, of course, Lloyd's of London, approached through a Lloyd's broker. In addition, most of the building societies and in particular the banks are now keen to sell you insurance – sometimes under their own 'brand', but often through their own formalised tie-ups.

But, as with insurances you are more used to buying, insurance companies vary a great deal in their premiums, their policy terms and conditions and, critically, in their promptness and fullness at claim time. Thus the best plan is not to go directly to a company (even if you already transact your car or life insurances with them), but to an insurance broker.

Insurance brokers receive their income from commissions from the insurance companies they represent, but they are generally independent of individual companies and thus reasonably impartial. In theory, a broker can deal with the full range of insurance companies and should be able to find the best (not necessarily the lowest) quote for you; in reality a broker is unlikely to vet the whole market just for you, and so you owe it to yourselves to use care in selecting one to act for your business. You can get the names and addresses of local firms from a number of sources e.g. Yellow Pages, Enterprise Agencies, or your accountant or solicitor. My advice would be to make sure that they are properly registered members of one of the professional bodies, especially BIIBA (the British Insurance and Investment Brokers' Association). If you have time, you should consider approaching three different firms of brokers to make recommendations for your business insurances, and then you should be confident of which one is best; as a rule of thumb, it is probably wise to select a firm that is big enough to have contacts in all the fields for which you might need cover (and big enough to exert pressure on your behalf when it comes to making a claim), but not so big that the relatively modest amounts of commission they will earn from your business will not motivate them to continue with a conscientious service to, for instance, remind you of renewals or help you monitor your full and actual insurance needs.

Most insurance companies now package covers together so that you get a basic level of insurance and then 'pick and choose' options to match your business's needs. Do be wary of buying more insurance than you realistically need by this method. If you can be bothered, your broker can quite often 'broke' you a more suitable package between companies. That's what he's there for – use him!

How much cover do you need?

I have just mentioned the possibility of over-insurance, but as you might imagine, it is far more common – and dangerous – to under-insure. Here, the most you can be paid in a claim is the amount of the sum insured – if that's insufficient, then tough! But do be aware of a standard practice in the insurance industry to apply 'Average'. If you are under-insured and you make a claim, then the pay-out will be reduced in proportion to the level of under-insurance – if your £40,000 workshop and machinery are only insured for £10,000, then the insurer will only pay out 10K/40K i.e. a quarter of each of your claims. Therefore, you really should work on the full replacement costs when you are arranging your insurances and your considerations should include the following (if they're relevant to your business):

1 **Buildings** – insure for the rebuilding value, not the market value; professional valuation is advisable. Take into account any possible increase in costs through delay, alteration in rebuilding design which could be requested by your local authority, architects, surveyors, consulting engineers, legal fees and the cost of debris removal.

2 **Contents and machinery** – furniture, fixtures, fittings and machines should be insured for their replacement value as new, in addition to:

   ● Documents, manuscripts, business books – their value as stationery plus the cost of rewriting.

   ● Computer systems records – their value as materials and the cost of labour plus computer time to reinstate.

   ● Unless insured elsewhere, directors' and employees' personal effects.

3 **Stock** (especially for shop policies) – as relevant, insure for the cost to you of manufacture or replacement value. Your policy can automatically allow for stock increases, for example in December and January and the 31 days prior to Easter Monday – consider whether this is sufficient or whether it would be better allowed for at different times of the year.

4 **Book debts** – should represent the maximum likely to be outstanding at any one time, including a suitable allowance for expansion of business, seasonal variations, inflation and VAT, but deducting an allowance for bad debts.

5 **Gross fees** (especially for office policies) – as you will have to use last year's figures, add a reasonable amount for expansion over the next 24 months. Remember you could have a claim towards the end of the period of insurance and need to have the following year's fees

replaced. Further, if you are insuring for increased cost of working you should take into account such things as expenditure incurred in fitting out temporary offices, removal costs and expenses, increased rent and rates and so on.

6 **Gross profit** (especially for small businesses) – this is calculated by deducting purchases from annual turnover. As you will have to use last year's figures as a basis for this calculation, you need to add a reasonable amount for business expansion over the next 24 months. This is in case you claim towards the end of the insurance period and need to replace the following year's profit.

Fig 3.8 All your plant and machinery should be suitably insured

I'll conclude this section with some general pointers on selecting business insurance: *every year* get at least three quotes – if not through three brokers as suggested, then at least approach three companies –

different firms have different expertise, rates and specialisations. Compare the premiums, the packages/covers, the pay-out records and the premium frequency – often for just a small loading you can help your business's cash flow by paying in monthly instalments instead of annually. Read the small print carefully – commercial insurance is a lot more thorough and fickle in both its proposal and payment procedures so you must be too if you're not going to leave yourself open to non-settlement of a claim.

Now, let's look more specifically at the types of insurance available to your business.

Insurance required by law and contract

1 Employers' liability – you must have insurance to pay out for your legal liability if one of your employees is injured, made ill or diseased as a result of working for you. The amount of cover is generally unlimited but must be at least £2 million, and if this sounds a lot just keep an eye on the newspapers to see how court settlements are rocketing both in value and frequency as the great British public become more litigation conscious like their American cousins. Also consider widespread incidence of newly recognised conditions like repetitive strain injury (RSI) – if you're an employer you can be sued! The law also requires you to exhibit a certificate of employers' liability insurance at each place of work.

2 Motor insurance – this will be more familiar to any of you with a car, but by law you must insure your liability to others (known as third party liability) which occurs because of a car crash or other motor vehicle accident. This includes death or injury to anybody (but not your employees while working, as they are covered by employer's liability insurance, as above) as well as damage to third party property including other vehicles. In addition you might want to add fire and theft cover, and if you want cover for accidental damage to your vehicles whoever is to blame, you need a fully comprehensive policy. Further, if your vehicles are going to be driven by various persons, make sure you get an 'all drivers' policy; if you are using your car as a minicab you'll need special 'hire and reward' cover.

If you use your private car or other vehicles for business purposes you may require an extension to your normal policy at extra cost, particularly if it's going to be used for sales-repping or delivery. Do be clear at proposal stage what the vehicle is likely to be used for as there are plenty of 'grey areas' in defining 'business purposes' and failure to honestly disclose details may mean that the insurance company will not pay out on your claim.

Finally, if your work involves a great deal of driving, insure for the loss of your driving licence which could otherwise mean the loss of your livelihood - the insurance cannot restore your licence, but it can supply the means to hire a chauffeur.

3 Engineering equipment – by law, certain equipment such as pressure vessels and lifting tackle, has to be inspected and certified to be safe on an annual basis. This insurance and maintenance is often combined within an 'engineering policy' covering all the plant and machinery used by a firm against risks such as collapse, explosion and breakdown.

4 Contractual obligations – if you use other people's property (e.g. under a lease or hire purchase agreement) or carry or store other people's goods, you may need to insure them. Study the contracts and take expert advice if necessary.

Essential insurance

1 Material loss/damage insurance against fire, theft and other perils – covers destruction of or damage to your buildings and contents through fire, and you can – at extra cost – extend the policy to cover other perils like storm, flood, subsidence, explosion, lightning, aircraft, impact, riot, civil commotion, malicious damage, burglary and so on. Note that the insurance definition of 'theft' involves force or violence, so theft policies do not automatically protect against loss due to the dishonesty of employees or other people entitled to be on the premises – for this you will need to extend the cover to 'fidelity insurance' (you may consider this 'highly desirable' rather than 'essential').

Some of the features of a business that should be covered are:

- The business premises, including site clearance/rebuilding costs at inflation-adjusted prices
- The contents, including fixtures/fittings, industrial plant, tools and other equipment
- The stock, including stock-in-trade and work-in-progress
- Goods on sub-contractors' premises.

2 Public liability – covers the firm's need to compensate third parties for injury, loss or damage sustained through the activities of your business or one of its employees while at work e.g. a labourer drops a brick on a passer-by's head. You should have cover for at least £500,000 for each claim against you and preferably for up to £1 million (possibly more if you do business in the USA). Extra slices of cover are not expensive, but again, expect the premium for this type of insurance to rise as consumers in the UK become more litigation conscious.

3 Product liability – covers you for claims which occur as a result of the goods you are producing, selling, servicing or repairing causing injury or damage (up to a limit each year) e.g. if you produced a chair which collapsed under a purchaser; perhaps a washing machine or TV you repaired subsequently gives an electric shock; a child may be injured or poisoned by a toy you made; or a car you repaired crashed and it could subsequently be proved to be down to your work. Goods must meet certain safety standards and the law can hold you responsible if yours don't. You may not need this kind of insurance if you provide a service or a product unlikely to cause any damage, but otherwise it's very wise to have it.

4 Professional indemnity – covers firms, partnerships and individuals whose business is to provide expert advice, and who may be faced with claims for damages sustained through their negligence or misconduct. Such claims are on the increase and so the cover is wise and, for some occupations, imperative. But be warned – the premiums can be exorbitant and can stop a new business in its tracks.

5 Key person insurance – in many businesses, one or two – sometimes more – people make an outstanding contribution to success. It may be through their particular knowledge, abilities,

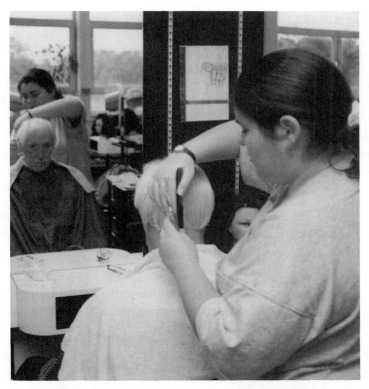

Fig 3.9 A business like this, operating in the high street, will have employers' liability and public liability cover

experience or contacts – or all of these. Or through their charisma, reputation, energy or sheer popularity – qualities which help win business and motivate staff. In small businesses such key persons will usually be owners or directors. Statistics show that one in every three company directors aged 40 will die before reaching age 65, and many more will be victims of ill-health or injury. When this happens it can dramatically slash profits and perhaps even threaten a business with extinction. It can create problems over the ownership and control of the business and it can reduce the business's ability to meet its commitments. Through key person insurance, you can insure for a significant sum – say, £250,000 – to be paid to your business in the event of a key person dying or becoming too permanently disabled to continue to work. To get cover you need to prove that the person's demise would cost your firm money but any settlement paid can, for instance, keep you in business; compensate you for loss of profits; give you a breathing space while you reorganise and / or find a suitable replacement; and save you from having to find a new credit line at a difficult time.

6 Director's share protection – provides for the shares of a director who dies to pass into the right hands. It makes sure that the family of the deceased director receives fair payment for his or her shares which saves them the problem of having to find an alternative buyer who may be utterly incompatible with the remaining directors or their plans. It can help avoid expensive and protracted litigation, and it protects cash flow and profits.

Incidentally, partnerships can experience similar problems and it is possible to arrange a suitable life assurance plan to avoid undue strain on the surviving partner(s) resources.

Fig 3.10 Your top designer – key person cover may be relevant

Highly desirable insurance

1 **Personal insurances** – you should make it a high priority to arrange a basic level of life assurance on either a 'term' or 'family income benefit' basis to alleviate financial hardship to your family in the event of your death. Sickness and accident insurance can pay either an income or a lump sum in the event of your incapacity to work; you might also consider permanent health insurance to cover 'permanent' rather than temporary incapacity to work. It is wise to arrange life and sickness insurance specifically to cover business loans. Private medical insurance is also a good precaution because it allows some control over the timing of any operations you might need, so that you can get back to your business quickly and efficiently. But moving back to more commercial issues . . .

2 **Loss of money insurance** – cash or near cash such as cheques, postal orders, postage stamps and credit card sales vouchers can be insured against theft from office or shop premises, or loss in transit – for instance you could be robbed while taking it to the bank. Clearly this cover is worth having if your takings are in cash, but otherwise probably not. Be aware too that insurers may insist on precautions, such as varying banking times or routes, or banking each day's takings in the bank's night safes. Insurance can be taken out to compensate an employee who is injured while being robbed of money.

Incidentally, firms who hold clients' money, such as travel and insurance *agents*, need an insurance *bond* to protect against loss if the business fails – bonding is actually compulsory for some kinds of agency.

3 **Goods in transit insurance** – covers loss or damage of your goods on the way to the customer, or to a subcontractor, or to the docks for shipment; in your own or someone else's vehicles, or some other means of delivery such as post. It can be simple insurance against collision, but an all risks policy that covers theft, negligence etc. is probably worth getting unless you do not sell your 'product' in this way.

4 **Specialised policies** – depending on the nature of the business, small firms may need additional specialised policies like:

- Glass breakage
- Frozen foods or other stock deterioration
- Business machines and equipment
- Agricultural and fish-farming operations

But remember, a material loss or damage claim will generally result in a loss greater than that of the equipment or stock lost, damaged or stolen . . .

Fig 3.11 Goods will need to be suitably covered whilst in transit
Source: Leyland Daf

5 Consequential loss (of gross profits) insurance – this provides cover if business is interrupted through damage to property by fire or other insured perils. It ensures that anticipated net profit is maintained, pays employees while laid off, and pays additional working costs if alternative facilities have to be used (Commercial Union chicken processing plant case). Usually you insure an amount related to your expected annual profits (but be careful if an established profit 'history' is required) and terms will be set according to your particular business. Whether this cover is worth getting depends on your business; if your business is small with few employees and you could easily run it from another premises (perhaps home), it may be enough to insure for the cost of finding somewhere else to carry on working, plus relocation costs, but often it is a worthwhile insurance to get.

6 Credit insurance – protects against non-payment of accounts by customers and is especially important for small firms who depend on just a very few customers. The firm must insure its whole credit turnover, not just selected doubtful accounts. The insurer often advises on credit control and normally you will still have to carry at least 10 per cent of the risk yourself; it is probable that you won't be able to get this kind of cover until you've been in business for quite some time. It's probably not worth getting this kind of cover if your business deals mainly in cash or payment on delivery, and for selling on credit terms. By the time you can get this kind of insurance you will be able to work out for yourself how likely a bad debts problem will be – it is likely to be better to operate good credit control or use a factoring service.

7 Directors' and officers' insurance – this cover is only relevant to company directors, who in many circumstances can be legally liable for an unlimited amount of damages. As a director, you have a duty to shareholders – even if they are just one or two people who you know well – and they can sue you. You have duties of skill and care to the company - and that can be capable of all sorts of interpretations. You have a duty under the increasingly more complicated Companies Acts and you may suffer a personal liability if the company goes bust, even if it is not your fault and you had no real say in the final decisions which broke the company.

The company itself can cover you to a certain extent, but the gap between that and full protection is wide – hence the need for 'D & O' insurance. Sun Alliance is one of the leaders in this field and they offer policies covering directors up to £5 million, or more if necessary. The policy doesn't cover dishonesty by self, but it will cover the cost of defending a claim for an illegal act and it will protect directors who have been victim to the dishonest acts of fellow board members.

8 Legal expenses – this insurance would enable you to pay for legal assistance if you are involved in a contractual or employment dispute, plus some other legal procedures. By becoming a member of the

Federation of Small Businesses (32 St Annes Road West, Lytham St. Annes, Lancashire FY8 1NY), you are automatically entitled to insurance cover up to £35,000 in these specific areas:

- Expenses of VAT tribunal cases
- Awards made by industrial tribunals
- Inland Revenue in-depth investigations and appeals against decisions under the 1985 Finance Act in respect of VAT.

Further legal expenses insurance includes assistance with Health & Safety Executive (HSE) cases, and also motoring prosecutions. A further benefit is a 24-hour telephone legal advice service. The FSB also runs a voluntary top-up scheme to supplement this basic legal cover.

Although there is a strong argument for joining the FSB or one of the other trade bodies for small business anyway (The Small Business Bureau, Suite 46, Westminster Palace Gardens, Artillery Row, London SW1P 1RR; The Forum of Private Business, Ruskin Chambers, Drury Lane, Knutsford, Cheshire WA16 6HA), it is probably not worth your while getting legal expenses insurance until later on. Most legal disputes are in the employment field, and it would be better to concentrate on getting well organised in this area to cut the risk of being taken to a tribunal charged with unfair dismissal. (An interesting scheme is Allianz Legal Protection's Lawplan which enables policyholders to pursue business-to-business debts. It also covers a wide variety of legal costs related to business activities, such as contract disputes, but your need for such cover depends on the nature of your business.)

'When you can afford it' insurance

Leaving these insurances to the end of the list doesn't mean that they are not important. Unless you're operating a 'cash cow', you would be wise to concentrate on building up your business to afford them first rather than spreading your initial resources too thin and putting the whole lot in unnecessary jeopardy through overstretched cash flow etc.

***Fig 3.12 A pension scheme for your key employees is
well worth considering***

1 Pensions – touched on in the next section on National Insurance,
the basic state pension is rather paltry and you really must make your
own private provision if you're to enjoy a comfortable retirement. To
this end it would be sensible to set up a small regular contribution
(monthly, quarterly or annually) into a plan as early as possible,
perhaps from Day 1. But do not be talked into large regular premiums
by an insurance salesman, only make significant contributions in
consultation with your accountant, and then, unless there is a very
good reason (e.g. to support a loan or as part of a small self-
administered scheme), only make top-up *single* premiums each year to
mop up otherwise taxable profits. Pension premiums attract tax relief
at the highest personal or corporate rate you pay and you can often
absorb very sizeable sums in this way by setting contributions against
profits and earnings over up to the past seven years.

Although regular pension premiums are good from a habit point of
view, they do generate substantial commission payments for the
salesman – this is OK if you maintain your payments for years, but if
you subsequently lapse your policy after only two or three years, it is
your fund which loses, rather than the salesman's commission income.

Single premiums give you greater control and less penalty providing you have the discipline to keep the money aside and pay them on a regular basis.

2 Additional life assurance – over and above your basic needs covered in the 'highly desirable' section. If you make arrangements for this through a 'Section 637' policy (or a company pension scheme), your premiums can also get tax relief at the highest rate that you or the company pay.

3 Savings plans, unit trusts, investment trusts, PEPs etc – make sure you can afford them!

For personal financial needs such as pensions, investments and life assurance you should definitely seek independent advice from an intermediary registered and licensed to sell the products of many companies rather than someone tied to just one company who is therefore only able to recommend from one company's product range. Independent intermediaries must be authorised by a self-regulatory organisation like FIMBRA – use them!

Clearly insurance for small business is a complex topic so the case for proper professional advice cannot be too strongly stated.

JULIAN CHILDS

Mainly Marketing

MAINLY MARKETING . . .
Insight   Inspiration   Implementation

The accountant's audit

The statutory audit, apart from establishing the financial accounts of a business, can be the foundation for a more wide-ranging review. In this case study, Grant Thornton reveals how the audit can explore the standing and likely needs of a business. Corporate finance issues are described along with a range of other financial services.

Grant Thornton ●

Grant Thornton is a leading international accounting firm. We provide a comprehensive range of business advisory services to a wide variety of clients – from private individuals to major companies.

Grant Thornton has 44 offices in the UK, providing complete business advisory teams, and every office is backed by the resources of Grant Thornton International, our worldwide network spanning over eighty countries. We provide clients with constructive, objective and professional advice to help them define and achieve their ambitions – both in the UK and overseas.

Overall responsibility for each of our client's affairs is taken by one partner, supported by a team of highly skilled advisers; together they will help interpret business needs, identify opportunities for growth, and minimise risks.

Audit – the core service

We believe that the wealth of information gathered each year during a statutory audit can prove invaluable to a company, providing an essential bedrock to major business planning. Many companies, however, overlook these opportunities. Audit is often the starting point of Grant Thornton's extensive range of business advisory services. We can look beyond the audit's basic task – reporting on a business's overall financial position – to its potential for evaluating management structure, tax arrangements, invoicing procedures, information and communications systems and its policies for buying and marketing.

In addition to providing an independent examination of a company's accounts, we can undertake a much wider-reaching process of investigation and analysis. We see audit as an interpretive tool for forward planning – not just a retrospective accounting review. Audit gives us a detailed knowledge of the workings of a business.

Grant Thornton's services include management advisory services, tax planning, corporate finance advice, IT consultancy and personal financial planning. All are designed to contribute to greater profitability and the growth of the business, and all can be individually tailored to suit specific business needs.

During the audit we will evaluate the company's accounting systems and internal controls. In our report to management we will comment on this evaluation, providing analysis and recommendations for possible improvements.

Our software specialists have developed a number of computer-based applications which we use during our audit. Taking data direct from the computer used by a business, it enables us to produce an analytical profile. We can compare this performance analysis to the mean of the relevant industry sector or to key competitors, and then report in tabular or graphic form. We can help to identify the key strengths or weaknesses of a business in relation to the market in which it operates.

With the depth of information gathered, we can identify existing or potential problems facing a company, and provide the right services to tackle them. We will also help a business to improve systems in order to make the company more efficient and profitable. And where we consider there is a risk, we will advise on how best to reduce the exposure.

Additional services

The Grant Thornton audit gives a detailed insight into how a business works. But what gives that knowledge real value is the opportunity for the owner to exploit the additional services that might be required.

Cash flow forecasts

We can help to prepare cash flow and profit projections to help managers plan capital expenditure and financing requirements for the following year. We can also assist in negotiations with the company's bank manager.

Corporate finance

At every stage of a company's life, from starting up to a flotation on the stock exchange, finance is the key to success: when and how to raise money; whether to acquire another business and how to pay for it; when to go public. Corporate finance decisions underpin the growth and development of the business.

However well someone knows their own business, they may be less confident where they have to make important decisions for the company involving, for example, raising money, buying or selling a business or issuing shares. An independent corporate finance specialist can help in development of a planned approach to achieving growth. A specialist, using his knowledge and experience of many types of commercial situation, can give objective and practical advice about the financing of a business.

At Grant Thornton we recognise that helping companies to make the right corporate finance decisions is vital. From the day-to-day problems of financial management to the longer term planning that shapes a company's future, we can help define corporate objectives:

- assist in preparing business plans;
- identify appropriate sources of finance;
- put together proposals for potential investors;
- negotiate terms of investment, acquisition or disposal;
- organise teams of professional advisers for share issues.

We provide a comprehensive corporate finance service that will take account of the business as a whole.

Compliance

An in-depth and detailed analysis of VAT and PAYE systems will enable a business to avoid costly penalties by complying with all appropriate government regulations.

Tax efficiency

Our corporate tax specialists can ensure that a company is benefiting from the most efficient tax structure. We can provide expert advice on foreign taxes and custom regulations, and through Grant Thornton International, co-ordinate activity with our offices in the countries concerned.

Grants review

With the help of our grants and business incentives service we can determine if a business qualifies for a local or national business incentive grant, and identify grant-aided opportunities for the purpose of expansion.

Personal financial planning for management

We can review the employee reward structure. Our personal financial planning specialists can help key personnel to maximise their earnings by advising them on investment, inheritance and settlement arrangements. Additionally, we can assist in the establishment of pension schemes for senior management and employees.

Management advisory service

In addition to our audit services, we provide a comprehensive range of advisory services designed to help a business develop, maximise efficiency and achieve long-term goals. We can help to develop and implement information technology, production and marketing strategies. Our specialists can also assist in reviewing, updating and installing the increasingly important 'quality systems' necessary for a business.

Confidence in the future

As a business grows and develops, the Grant Thornton audit enables us to tailor our advisory services to match changing requirements, helping a business to grow and prosper. In short, Grant Thornton helps a business become more effective. The range of services we provide enables business people to plan ahead with confidence, and exercise greater control and direction over their business and its future.

Grant Thornton, the UK member firm of Grant Thornton International, is authorised by the Institute of Chartered Accountants in England and Wales to carry on investment business.

Vehicle and asset finance

Lombard Business Finance provides leasing and hire purchase facilities to fund all types of business assets, from car fleets and commercial vehicles to plant and machinery. In this case study Lombard describes a range of funding options and how they meet the needs of the business community.

BUSINESS FINANCE

Lombard Business Finance is part of Lombard North Central PLC, the UK's largest finance house. Our beginnings go back to 1861 when, as The North Central Wagon Company, we hired wagons to railway companies.

Today we are part of Natwest Group with 4,300 employees controlling assets in excess of £9 billion. Each week Lombard North Central PLC advances around £100 million to customers large and small through three specialist divisions: Business, Personal and Motor Finance.

What is asset finance?

Principally it is a method of funding business related assets where the security is considered to be the asset that is being funded.

Whichever form of asset funding the customer decides on the repayment normally commences with a deposit or advance rental and the capital and interest is repayable by monthly or quarterly payments over an agreed period of time. The interest element can usually be fixed or variable at the outset.

There are two basic asset funding facilities: Leasing and Hire Purchase (sometimes called Lease Purchase).

With *leasing* the leasing company buys the equipment and hires it back to the customer. The finance company takes the tax allowances and remains 'the owner' throughout the agreement. When the lease is completed the equipment is sold, *to a third party*, and the customer will receive most of the sales proceeds as a rebate of rentals. Because the leasing company benefits from the tax allowances the rentals are normally very attractive. The customer never owns a leased asset.

What are the benefits of asset finance?

1 It preserves cash flow.

2 It is a committed term funding facility.

3 Buying equipment at today's prices and repaying out of tomorrow's income is an effective funding arrangement.

4 Repayments can be arranged to match depreciation and customer cash flow requirements.

5 Leasing can maximise the tax breaks that are available.

6 Credit facilities are straightforward and simple to establish and rarely require any collateral security, apart from the assets to be funded.

The traditional asset funding instruments are:

Lease/hire purchase

A fixed term capital and interest repayment facility whereby at the end of the agreement the customer may exercise an option to purchase the asset. This facility is suitable for most kinds of identifiable business assets and ideal for funding long life assets. For assets financed by this method, businesses will normally be able to claim the writing down allowances on the cash price and offset the interest charges against taxable profits. Repayments can be structured monthly, quarterly or even annually to match cash flow requirements.

Leasing

Generally a more suitable option for asset funding where use is more important than ownership. The ownership of the asset is retained by

FRUITS OF VICTORY!

Pictured above Mr Clive Mannering (right), Group Financial Director, J.P. Fruit Distributors, Dartford with Mark Allen, Account Executive, Lombard Business Finance. Mark, who is based at our London South Business Centre at Bromley, was happy to transact a £1.7 million Lease Purchase Facility to finance 38 banana ripening rooms for the company. Needless to say, Lombard are always glad to be of service to companies with this kind of growth potential!

Source: Lombard

the leasing company with use of the asset being passed to the customer (the lessee) for an agreed period of time. With the leasing company purchasing the equipment and taking the tax allowances, leasing can become an extremely efficient means of asset funding. For most businesses, lease rentals are allowable against taxable profits, in line with the business's normal depreciation policy. This facility is suitable for all types of assets including motor cars which are subject to special rules.

The two principal forms of leasing are:

Finance leases

Finance leases are suitable for virtually all types of plant, machinery, vehicles and computers. The customer pays the full cost of capital and interest through regular rentals. However, in many cases, when the assets are sold the customer benefits from the majority of the sales proceeds by way of a rebate of rentals. Rentals can include fixed or variable rate interest. Normally a finance lease is 'on balance sheet' for accounting purposes.

Operating leases

For accounting purposes, this is a lease that does not meet the requirements of a finance lease. It is usual for the leasing company (the lessor) to assume the risks and rewards of ownership in such an agreement. The disposal of the asset at the end of the agreement is normally the responsibility of the lessor. Initially this facility was available for vehicles only but nowadays is suitable for a whole range of assets. This is the case particularly when the lessor, like Lombard, has its own asset management unit. An operating lease has the added attraction of being treated as 'off balance sheet' subject to approval by the customer's auditors.

Finance is a heavily regulated industry and Lombard must adhere to the stringent controls and policies set by the Inland Revenue, The Bank of England, Office of Fair Trading and other regulatory authorities who define and set the limits as to the amounts of capital allowance, depreciation, tax exemption and other allowances a company may claim and the type of financial agreement terms we may use. Indeed, many of Lombard's facilities incorporate these tax allowances, enabling smaller businesses to avail of these legal concessions that they would otherwise not be entitled to. Much of this is due to the sheer scale of Lombard's operations as a business in its own right and the fact that we purchase so that others can use.

Through its membership of the Finance and Leasing Association and other organisations, Lombard regularly lobbies government and other regulatory bodies to instil economic growth.

With 28 dedicated business centres, Lombard has over a quarter of a million current business accounts nationwide funding everything from cars to computers and machine tools to medical equipment. Contracts can range in value from as little as one thousand pounds for office equipment such as PCs and photocopiers to tens of millions of pounds for assets such as factory production lines, civil aircraft and even satellites. Each agreement is unique; a personal bespoke arrangement between customer and funder.

Lombard Business Finance
TONY TAYLOR, *Senior Manager, Marketing*
PAT GALLIGAN, *Marketing Controller*
IAN ISAAC, *Senior Manager, London South*
SHEENA LOTT, *Sales Co-ordinator, London South*

Part 4

Illustrative Studies

These studies, which are provided to facilitate learning, describe imaginary businesses.

The guidance provided by BTEC for Element 12.2 was the initial motivation behind their inclusion. Students following the RSA programme should also find them useful.

Each study considers a growing business and reveals how the financial services industry has served its evolving needs. Each organisation ultimately finds itself at a critical point, and you may wish to consider its future.

'The Video Shop'

'The Video Shop' based in Swindon is a small store offering tapes for hire run by a sole proprietor. This is her story.

I have now been in business for five years offering a wide range of films for hire to the public. I operate from a compact retail outlet and typically have over 1,200 titles in stock.

The shop is open seven days a week from 11 a.m. to 9 p.m., and is staffed by myself and three part-time assistants. Our aim is to provide not just the latest releases but also a wide range of back catalogue family films and cinema classics.

Turnover of the former is high in the early weeks following release, but typically tails off after a couple of months or so. I try to manage the stock levels of new titles carefully to ensure that tapes are not languishing on the shelves as demand reduces. If too much capital is tied up in under-used stock, not only is it not generating revenue, it is also costing me money as I am borrowing from the bank at the moment.

I control the stock of video tapes and the store membership records by using a computer package. I could not afford to purchase the hardware and special software package outright so I decided to lease it. I make regular, in fact monthly, payments to the supplier by direct debit from my bank account.

I have an arrangement with three nearby convenience stores to provide them with stock for rental. As titles are requested less frequently in my outlet I transfer them to these shops, and utilisation is therefore maintained. We share the rental proceeds, and I retain ownership.

The store contents are fully insured through my insurance broker who, coincidentally, operates from a small office above it. We both therefore, as leaseholders, have the same landlord. I have the shop on a fifteen-year lease with three-yearly reviews – so the next review is in a year's time. I pay the landlord a quarterly rent in advance by standing order from my bank account. The lease requires that I pay for adequate buildings insurance on the premises, as ground floor occupier, but this policy is actually arranged by the freeholder.

The front window – a large pane of plate glass – requires special cover which is provided through my contents policy. I naturally have employer liability and public liability – both are essential.

Most of my turnover is in cash so I regularly use my bank's night safe to deposit money out of hours. I am very excited by a new product, Mondex, which was created by the NatWest Group. It is designed as an alternative to cash, and I hope to start using it on a trial basis shortly. I think my customers will like it. I do accept credit and payment cards but most people prefer using cash on payments of less than £5.00.

I am aiming to diversify somewhat next month by offering video equipment for hire. I anticipate offering VHS cameras for daily rental to those who know how to use them. Alternatively, for special events and those needing guidance I will offer a full service of camera and operator. I hope that events such as weddings will generate plenty of bookings.

The new camera equipment is actually owned by a friend with whom I am about to go into partnership. Our solicitor is shortly to draw up a suitable partnership agreement. We will all have to consider the existing value of my video business and the cost of the new assets being brought in to finalise this. I will also have to amend both my insurance and my banking arrangements. The new side to the business will have to be appropriately advertised so I will hope to extend my bank overdraft to enable this to happen. A visit to my bank to discuss the expansion with their small business adviser really is the next stage.

My new partner is a computer expert and believes that we should hire out not just video tapes but also computer games. If we decide to take the shop next door we would have the space to retail a large selection of video tapes as well as enter the computer games market. Such a move will make fresh demands on capital. Although we could afford to refurbish the new shop, we would not be able to afford the stock at the moment! To ensure that the business is viable we will have to draw up a new business plan and somehow inject more funds into the firm.

'Microflight UK Ltd'

'Microflight UK Ltd' is a private limited company which imports kitplanes from the USA. It is run by a family team – this is their story.

My brother and I started this business as a partnership twelve years ago, providing maintenance support to a range of light aircraft.

The growing interest in light aviation, and in particular microlights – very lightweight one- and two-seat machines – led us towards expansion by becoming distributors for a range of American-designed machines.

Whilst we were negotiating the UK franchise some six years ago over in the USA we realised it was an appropriate time to cease operating as a partnership and form a private limited company. On returning to the

Fig 4.1 'The first machine we imported nearing completion'

UK we visited both our accountant and solicitor who guided us through the process. A subsequent trip to our bank to amend account details was also necessary. Six months after the original transatlantic trip we were back in Florida finalising our deal with the manufacturer.

Our initial contract required us to pay in advance for the kits, which were naturally priced in US dollars. As we always knew this was to be the case we had sought advice from our bank manager as to how to handle the situation to our advantage. We discussed a variety of possible options – an overdraft or a loan seemed the most likely solution.

Often in business you need a little luck. A senior pilot for a major international airline was just nearing the end of his flying career and had approached us to refurbish his own two-seater plane for use in his retirement. His early retirement package provided him with a substantial lump sum – over £75,000 – and he decided, on hearing of our plans, to become both an investor in our operation and an adviser to us on a one day a week basis (I was later told that such investors are known as business angels!). This cash injection gave us the ability to buy currency and therefore order machines for shipment to us here in Wales.

His cash enabled our local bank to buy the US dollars, which it then transferred out to another bank in Miami. Two or three months later the kits we had ordered arrived here in South Wales. Sending out cash in advance is not always advisable, but I had known the American manufacturers for some years and trusted them. After a few months I began using documentary credits with Bills of Exchange on the advice of my bank manager. This was due to the increase in demand in the UK for our products combined with pressure on our cash flow as we improved our premises.

A documentary credit drawn up by our UK bank in favour of the American company enabled us to purchase more kits. The Americans received a Bill of Exchange, guaranteed by our bank, to be paid after ninety days had passed. We always sold the kits for sterling, and asked our customers to put down a 10 per cent deposit when they ordered one. The remaining 90 per cent had to be cleared through our bank account prior to the buyer taking delivery, so sometimes we had all the money before the ninety days were up!

As you can imagine, the fluctuation of sterling against the US dollar could have caused us a few problems. The first time we purchased kits the exchange rates did not matter too much as we knew the sales revenue would cover costs so that our anticipated profit margin did materialise. Our business angel could see that in the future, life might not be so easy. A weak sterling could lead to us having to charge too much for the kit in the UK. Price cutting to maintain sales would leave us no way to cover shipping costs as well as our UK overheads.

In 1993 we decided to set a price for the kits in the UK of £9,750 for a standard specification machine. Since then we have always agreed forward rates on the currency purchased from our bank, so we know that we can aim for a modest profit. Customers get a fair deal as they do not have to worry about specific exchange rates when they actually take the purchasing decision.

Fig 4.2 'We display machines at exhibitions and rallies'

In 1995 we became Northern European distributors so we now sell kits throughout France, Belgium and the Netherlands. When overseas buyers purchase from us they ask their own banks to provide cheques (drafts) drawn in sterling on a UK bank. This means that they have to change from their currency (French francs, Belgian francs, Dutch guilders) into sterling, and I am not forced to take an exchange risk. When they order parts with their credit cards the process is simple as I quote a sterling price which is converted into their currency by their credit card company. I wonder when all of this will be simplified by the introduction of a single European currency?

I now employ seven staff as well as Peter, our business angel, and they are paid monthly by direct transfers between my business account at the bank and their own accounts. My accountant takes care of all the sums – ensuring that they are sent the right amount after the appropriate deductions have been made.

Our future plans depend on the state of the market in Europe. We would like to design our own machines and sell them throughout Europe and North America. Such a project would require a substantial injection of capital and involve some risk. The decision to expand in such a way will not therefore be taken lightly. Both our bank manager and our accountant will need to be involved in the planning.

'Advanced Studies Plc'

Although there is an element of good fortune in this story it is really one of cautious continuity over a long period of time. It is told by the Company Secretary.

I have been employed by 'Advanced Studies' for over thirty years and have witnessed substantial growth combined with one or two setbacks.

Advanced Studies' core business these days is in the motor trade. We run seven main dealerships retailing the cars of five major manufacturers. Furthermore we operate three used car outlets. We also have a not insubstantial property portfolio generating rental income.

This position of strength in the region did not however arise overnight! Various takeovers proved necessary and fruitful: some closures meant that commercial properties had to be rebuilt, refurbished, re-let or released. Our bank frequently helped finance such developments, often securing their advances through other properties in our ownership. We have kept our professional advisers busy over the years.

All of these changes left a mixture of assets in a variety of names. One prominent company we took over happened to be established with a £50,000 issued and paid up capital and this proved to be a suitable 'vehicle' for grouping under a new name and bringing all of the business into one holding.

I should mention that one large closure, adjoining an acquired defunct cinema with car park, became (for us) a major reconstruction job producing an edge-of-town supermarket where we have remained freeholders. The rental income from it provides a valuable boost to our cash flow even now.

In the mid-1980s, as the economy boomed, it seemed that further expansion beyond our own financial resources was imminent, and we had informal discussions with two merchant banks in the City. One was a clearing bank recommendation, the other the choice of our accountants.

We felt at the time that 'going public' would be necessary at some stage but we have always aimed to proceed at our own pace, choosing the time rather than be pressured at an inopportune moment.

We considered risk management and systems in a general way and learned what was expected of us. As it turned out we did not then press ahead with a flotation and it was as well for us that we were cautious.

Fig 4.3 'We recently commissioned extensive new workshop facilities'

Apart from the new car franchises, where cars are financed under somewhat complex arrangements with the manufacturers, we handle a lot of the up-market previously-owned models. These call for much capital outlay, and have to be monitored and controlled carefully. If we have not sold a particular vehicle after two or three months we often have to consider shifting it through an auction. One of our smaller companies specialised in 'exotic' sports models and that one ultimately failed.

When we recovered we did, through our suitably capitalised company, convert to 'Plc'. In 1989 we actually became a public company but without a stock market listing: that is to say we became an unlisted public limited company. No shareholder changes arose through this: if and when we do go public that will be a job for a registrar – probably a service arrangement with a subsidiary of our high street bank.

Our accountants provided the required audited accounts and financial statements and documents back in 1989 and we will need their support again in the near future. Our next step, as we look forward with renewed optimism, is AIM, the new Alternative Investment Market. This we hope will fund our expansion through to the end of the century. What better way to progress to full public status?

Part 5

Assignments

This section of detailed assignments is designed to complement Parts 2, 3 and 4. Students will be given the opportunity to build and demonstrate their knowledge on the range of financial services, and how they meet business needs.

The following assignments provide opportunities with respect to the range of performance criteria of your chosen course, and whichever you undertake will reflect your own local facilities and market conditions.

The assignments

1 **Bancassurance** – an article for a business magazine explaining what this term means in the 1990s.

2 **Banks and small businesses** – a briefing pack on six key products/services.

3 **The college/school assignment** – consideration of college/school as a medium-sized business and consumer of a host of financial services.

4 **The company assignment** – a review of services used by a Public Limited Company.

5 **The *Financial Times*** – a study of the businessman's tool.

6 **A new product** – an in-depth recommendation of a new product to an actual local business.

7 **A real protection** – a presentation of a product, policy or service which might really protect a business from some form of risk.

8 **Who should I turn to?** – a study of key providers, to enable you to give a talk to a small business club.

9 **Experiencing financial services** – a five-day work experience placement in the financial services sector.

10 **The Financial Services Exhibition** – a finale to the year.

Undertaking assignments

Each assignment is designed to stimulate students in a different way. Various aspects of the financial services industry are considered, with the tasks set enabling the learner to undertake worthwhile investigations leading to the generation of real evidence of understanding. By following a simple and consistent format the assignments are approachable, yet open to adaptation to suit your own needs.

The assignments are introduced briefly, so that the learner can begin to appreciate their focus. Tasks are then set, to give direction towards the compilation of material appropriate to a financial services portfolio. The purpose follows, in order to link the tasks to the performance criteria relevant to the programme being followed. The performance criteria grid serves as a guide, but should not be considered in isolation from the awarding bodies' evidence indicators.

Whether you are following a BTEC or RSA programme, you will find these assignments worthy of integration into a teaching schedule. However, local market conditions and your own preferences as tutor (or learner) will be of relevance when making a selection.

As the assignments are presented in a concise format they are open to amendment. The ultimate level of each one can be altered through the addition of extra tasks, or simply by demanding more depth in the work undertaken. Furthermore, some may be changed from being set for an individual into a group task.

As your GNVQ programme evolves, opportunities should be sought to integrate different units, options and subject areas. You may, therefore, wish to jointly develop these assignments with other tutors with an aim of achieving additional performance criteria.

Remember, as the study programme comes to an end individual students will need to be guided towards the completion of their own portfolios and will, therefore, have priorities to concentrate on.

Bancassurance

Introduction

Banks, insurance companies and assurance companies have been in existence for years. Many in fact trace their histories back over the centuries, and have a proud tradition in having met the particular needs of businessmen over this time. However, a new breed of financial services provider is beginning to emerge at the end of the twentieth century. The term to describe this type of company is *Bancassurance*.

Task

You are to submit an article suitable for publication to the editor of a new publication. This new monthly magazine is to be aimed at the business sector, so your article needs to appeal to a broad readership. Company directors, small businessmen and a host of professionals are likely to subscribe to it. Your title is *Bancassurance – a new trend in providing for business needs*.

Remember, it should be typed, logical, and appropriate. You have been advised that a 1,000 word limit applies and are asked to supply two suitable illustrations.

Possible performance criteria	
BTEC	RSA
12:1/3, 4 12:2/3 12:3/3, 4	11 :1/2, 4, 5

Purpose

The aim of this article is to guide the potential reader around this topic, which is of key relevance to the future of the financial services sector in the UK. Most readers are likely to be customers of the Bancassurance type of company already, or will be the target of them as they gear up their marketing campaigns.

Banks and small businesses

Introduction

Banks view the small business sector of the economy as a key market segment to which they can deliver products of value. Over recent years they have striven to enhance the way they 'offer' their products to make them more appealing. Part of this process has encompassed the creation of small business packs indicating the breadth of a bank's product range.

Task

You are to provide a briefing pack to guide a businessman, in respect of six key products or services. This pack is to contain fact sheets for each product, indicating its features and benefits. It is most important, however, that the pack also explains the relevance of the products to a small business, and doesn't just reiterate the information provided by the banks themselves. Your briefing pack can be designed for the small business area in general, or a specific market sector, such as retail, manufacturing or services.

Possible performance criteria	
BTEC	RSA
12:1/1, 2, 3, 4 12:2/1, 3 12:3/1, 2, 3, 4	11:1/1, 2 11:3/1, 2, 3, 4

Purpose

The aim of this pack is to provide a guide to the small businessman, which combines clarity with relevance. The pack, if created around a diverse range of half a dozen products and services, should be a useful aid to decision making.

The college/school assignment

Introduction

With the increasing trend towards grant maintained schools and independent colleges, it is certainly not artificial to look upon one as a medium sized business enterprise. Such an organisation utilises a diverse range of financial services, and is likely to be reviewing and expanding its needs constantly.

Task

Produce a study of the range of financial servicing used by your place of education. You may wish to group the type of product by considering the type of need it fulfils. Alternatively, consider the provider and categorise on this basis from your knowledge of financial services. From this you may be able to identify products/services which, though not currently used, would actually fulfil a real need. Make recommendations on such issues accordingly. The choice of provider should be justified if access to the relevant information is available.

Possible performance criteria	
BTEC	RSA
12:1/1, 2, 3, 4 12:2/1, 2, 3 12:3/1, 2, 3, 4	11:1/1, 2 11:3/1, 2, 3, 4

Purpose

The aim of this assignment is for the learner to consider a business of which they are a client or customer. Some of the business needs, therefore, reflect the way they utilise school/college facilities. The report must combine factual accuracy with a genuine understanding of a range of products/services. Some of these needs will be satisfied internally, whilst others will be taken care of by external companies.

The company assignment

Introduction

It is likely that a 'Footsie' company will be chosen for this study, i.e. one of the hundred largest companies which make up the Financial Times – Stock Exchange 100 Index. The choice may best be directed towards manufacturing or retailing, rather than the service sector. Many of the top UK companies have balance sheets as good as, or superior to, the main providers of financial services in the UK, and therefore have the ability to serve their own needs rather than utilise the products of others. The starting point for this project will be the securing of the latest company report of your chosen company.

Task

You are to study a major UK PLC of your choice, which is likely to be a *Footsie* representative, but obviously should be outside the financial service sector. By carefully examining its latest annual report provide a summary of the financial services and providers it utilises. Some of these will be stated, while for others you will have to conclude likely examples from an understanding of their business operations. Finally, make recommendations as to any other services/products which you believe it could employ for its benefit, especially regarding the use of schemes which are new to the market-place.

Possible performance criteria	
BTEC	RSA
12:1/1, 2, 3, 4 12:2/1, 2, 3 12:3/1, 2, 3, 4	11:1/1, 2 11:3/1, 2, 3, 4

Purpose

By considering a major company conclusions may well be drawn in respect of the great competition to provide financial services in the UK to major corporate consumers. As many *Footsie* companies trade internationally the range of providers and relevant products will have a significant breadth. (As part of the debrief in class the companies investigated can be compared and contrasted and further conclusions drawn.)

The *Financial Times*

Introduction

The *Financial Times* is delivered each working day to thousands of businesses throughout the UK. It can genuinely be regarded as a tool to be used, but for the businessman to get the best out of it, it needs to be understood – it deserves an instruction manual!

Task

Listed below is a selection of key topics of critical importance to businesses which relate to the financial services industry in some way:

- The cost of borrowing money
- The returns on investments
- Latest trends in financial services
- New financial services/products
- Financial services advertising
- Prices: shares, futures, currencies etc.
- Latest news on legislation of financial services

Incorporate these, and perhaps two or more of your own choosing, into a succinct guide on how to use the *Financial Times*. The format needs to be more than just an index, as each topic needs an introduction before the role of the *Financial Times* is considered.

Possible performance criteria	
BTEC	RSA
12:1/1, 3, 4 12:2/1 12:3/3, 4	11:1/1, 2, 3, 4, 5 11:3/1, 2

Purpose

The aim of this assignment is for the learner to first become comfortable with the layout and content of the *Financial Times*. For the purpose of this assignment aim to consult a Tuesday, Wednesday, Thursday or Friday edition. The Monday edition has a somewhat different balance as it follows a non-working day when, therefore, the UK Financial Market has not been active. The Saturday edition is really a broader publication, as it endeavours to entertain the weekend readership and bears Friday's news – perhaps a less significant day with regard to news unfolding in the business sector. The ultimate aim is to create a document which can help the businessman get the most from this important publication.

(How much does the *Financial Times* cost? Many college/school bookshops are able to offer it with a substantial discount (at a special student rate), if they order a certain quantity (30 daily). If you feel this is appropriate, contact your bookshop/newstrade distributor. This discount offer runs for a limited period.)

A new product

Introduction

Different parts of the financial services industry have to produce new products, or enhance existing ones, to ensure that they survive and prosper. Companies functioning in an increasingly competitive world will either embrace or ignore these opportunities depending on their potential.

Task

You need ideally to select a new product or service that has recently been launched. In the absence of such innovations coming to the market, an existing one can be selected (in which case it must be considered in the context of a business which is not presently a consumer).

Describe the product and its supplier in terms of its features and benefits. Its relevance to different types of business can then be appreciated. Select a local small business as a potential customer and present your argument for it to become a user.

Possible performance criteria	
BTEC	RSA
12:1/1, 2, 3, 4 12:2/1, 3 12:3/1, 2, 3, 4	11:1/1, 2, 3, 5 11:3/1, 2, 3, 4

Purpose

By considering real products, real suppliers, and real potential consumers, a genuine business decision can be contemplated. Regulations and constraints concerning the sale of such products will be considered. If the selected business decides to proceed then an introduction to the provider can actually be made! By reviewing the findings of the class a broad range of products/services can be discussed.

A real protection

Introduction

Risk management is often poorly undertaken by businesses in the UK. By considering typical commercial risks a recommendation for a specific policy, product or service, appropriate to a chosen business, can be made.

Task

Initially the issues of risk management are to be explained by the learner. A specific example must then be explored in detail with a reasoned argument leading to a conclusion that an individual business should invest its resources in a selected product.

Possible performance criteria	
BTEC	RSA
12:1/1, 2, 4 12:2/1, 2, 3 12:3/1, 2, 3, 4	11:1/1, 2 11:3/1, 2, 3, 4

Purpose

The end result of this assignment should be that a business considers the recommendation sensible and realistic, in which case the learner has had the quality of their proposal confirmed. The actual purchasing decision may lead to an investment internally on further resources, or externally involving an independent provider.

Who should I turn to?

Introduction

With the financial services sector becoming increasingly competitive, it is vital that businesses shop around for the best value. For a small business engrossed in survival or expansion such a time consuming proposition may not be immediately appealing. Membership of a local Small Business Club may, for them, be one solution towards making the process simpler.

Task

You are to prepare for a presentation to your local Small Business Club. The title of your contribution is

> THE KEY PROVIDERS OF FINANCIAL SERVICES

and, subject to your local circumstances, this can be delivered as:

1 a ten-minute individual presentation, or

2 a one-hour presentation delivered by a group of between four to six persons.

Purpose

Although ten minutes on your own may sound daunting the critical issue is, in reality, adequate preparation. For this assignment the students will at least submit the evidence of their preparation and any notes and handouts for the session. You may wish to actually proceed with the presentations, in class to each other, to another college/school group, or even to the local Small Business Club itself!

Possible performance criteria	
BTEC	RSA
12:1/3, 4 12:2/2, 3 12:3/1, 2, 3, 4	11:1/2, 4, 5 11:3/1

Experiencing financial services

A five-day work experience placement in the financial services sector

Introduction

The financial services industry is a key employer, in which a student may seek full-time employment in due course. The breadth of potential placements is considerable, with banks, insurance companies, and various specialist financial services providers being represented nationwide.

Tasks

The provision in this text of a set task is, I believe, inappropriate. The first responsibility for the learner must be the securing of a valid placement. The student must, therefore, investigate the local environment and select a potential position. The written request for a five-day opportunity must be coupled with an up to date CV. A formal interview for the placement is appropriate, and the applicant's availability to attend one must be ensured. The precise role of the week should be negotiated with the 'employer' to reflect local conditions, opportunities, preferences and student needs.

Purpose

A careful consideration of relevant performance criteria must be undertaken to make sure that the placement offers both a valuable experience and the opportunity for portfolio compilation. The learner must balance the value of being in a work environment against evidencing performance criteria. The five days are precious, and portfolio evidence can always be generated later.

Possible performance criteria	
BTEC	RSA
The student and tutor should consider their aims before the placement commences. The generation of evidence can be at the placement and subsequent to it.	

The financial services exhibition

Introduction

This exhibition has the potential to be an impressive finale to the course. Book your hall and display screens early to make sure that the event can be planned and executed successfully. Aim to involve other students at college/school and the local financial services sector.

Task

Exhibitions need to be planned professionally! Consider the following points, that the group of learners will have to handle:

- Marketing
- Physical resources
- Exhibition content
- Exhibition duration
- Sponsorship
- Opening ceremony
- Invitations
- Prizegiving

This list is not exhaustive – and one of the key tasks is the successful organising of the actual project.

The exhibition layout detailed below is only a guide, and in reality your own presentation must reflect your objectives.

Each display area will aim to describe the product, the service, and the industry, as appropriate. Informative handouts are worthwhile, as they can form part of a portfolio of evidence. The exact format of the exhibition is down to the exhibitors. You may wish to concentrate on products, or alternatively on the providers. A mix of both is also appropriate. By incorporating a display on Advanced GNVQs and a survey centre to gauge visitors' views, the exhibition broadens its scope (and some planning for next year is undertaken).

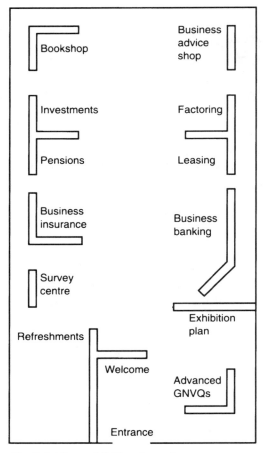

Fig 5.1 The exhibition layout

If you have courses doing small business enterprise projects 'subcontract' the refreshments and other opportunities, like an exhibition video or a bookshop, to them.

Possible performance criteria	
BTEC	RSA
All	All

Purpose

This exhibition is obviously a heavy commitment, but highly realistic and valuable. Students will probably work in teams of two to five persons and will clearly wish to enlist the help of local financial services providers. Local financial services companies can be invited to attend and view, as can the small business community. If the event is well organised it can become a satisfying day for all concerned. The potential to provide a prize for the most informative display is tempting, and this can be funded by the college / school sponsorship, or even an entrance fee! Do promote the exhibition to other courses at college / school as its content may be relevant to a variety of them.

(N.B. If you have never undertaken a project such as this before, and perhaps feel the outline here is over ambitious, consider using a large room and having poster displays within it. The challenge to reveal an understanding of the financial services industry still exists, and therefore the project retains its value.)

Part 6

Additional Sources of Information

This section provides the student with a range of information sources. It is not designed to be exhaustive, as part of the philosophy of the Vocational A level is that students themselves learn to investigate and to gather and sift information.

Useful addresses

For individual associations and institutes, see under appropriate title of body, e.g. British Insurers, Association of.

Bank of England
Threadneedle Street, London EC2R 8AH

Banking Information Service
10 Lombard Street, London EC3V 9EL

Banking Ombudsman
Citadel House, 5–11 Fetter Lane, London EC4 1BR

British Bankers Association
10 Lombard Street, London EC3V 9EL

British Factors and Discounters, Association of
1 Northumberland Avenue, London WC2N 5BW

British Insurance and Investment Brokers' Association
14 Bevis Marks, London EC3A 7NT

British Insurers, Association of
51 Gresham Street, London EC2V 7HQ

British Venture Capital Association
3 Catherine Place, London SW1E 6DX

Building Societies Association
3 Savile Row, London W1X 1AF

Confederation of British Industry
103 New Oxford Street, London WC1A 1DU

Chartered Accountants, Institute of
Chartered Accountants Hall, Moorgate Place, London EC2P 2BJ

Chartered Insurance Institute
31 Hillcrest Road, South Woodford, London E18 2JP

Chartered Surveyors, Royal Institute of
12 Great George Street, London SW1P 3AD

Chartered Secretaries and Administrators, Institute of
16 Park Crescent, London W1N 4AH

FIMBRA
Hartsmere House, Hartsmere Road, London E14 4AB

Government Actuary's Department
22 Kingsway, London WC2 B6LE

HMSO Books Publications Centre
51 Nine Elms Lane, London SW8 5DT

IMRO
Broadwalk House, 5 Appold Street, London EC2A 2LL

Institute of Management
Cottingham Road, Corby, Northants NN17 1TT

Institute of Linguists
24A Highbury Grove, London N5 2EA

Insurance Brokers' Registration Council
15 St Helens Place, London EC3A 6DS

Insurance Ombudsman Bureau
City Gate One, 135 Park Street, London SE1 9EA

International Chamber of Commerce (UK)
Centre Point, New Oxford Street, London WC1

LAUTRO
Centre Point, 103 New Oxford Street, London WC1A 1QH

Law Society
113 Chancery Lane, London WC2A 1PL

LIFFE
Cannon Bridge, London EC4R 3XX

Pension Schemes Office (IR)
Lynwood Road, Thames Ditton, Surrey KT7 0DP

Pension Schemes Registry (DSS)
PO Box 1NN, Newcastle upon Tyne NE99 1NN

Pensions Information Centre
51–55 Gresham Street, London EC2

Pensions (Occupational) Advisory Service
11 Belgrave Road, London SW1V 1RB

Pensions (Occupational) Board (DSS)
PO Box 2EE, Newcastle upon Tyne NE99 2EE

Pensions Ombudsman
11 Belgrave Road, London SW1V 1RB

Registrar of Companies
Companies House, Crown Way, Maindy, Cardiff CF4 3UZ

Registry of Friendly Societies
15–17 Great Marlborough Street, London W1V 2AX

Securities and Futures Authority Ltd
The Stock Exchange, Old Broad Street, London EC2N 1HP

Securities and Investment Board
2–14 Bunhill Row, London EC1Y 8RA

Stock Exchange, (The)
Throgmorton Street, London EC2N 1HP

Useful publications

The following journals and magazines cover current developments in the financial services sector:

The Banker	*Investors' Chronicle*
Business Age	*Money Management*
Business Franchise	*Money Observer*
Economist	*What Investment*
Enterprise	

The following professional institutes publish journals for members:

The Chartered Accountants in England and Wales	*Accountancy*
The Chartered Institute of Secretaries and Administrators	*Administrator*
The Chartered Institute of Bankers	*The Chartered Banker, CIB News, Banking World*

(NB *Banking World* ceased publication in June 1995 but copies may be retained in libraries and be useful for research.)

The Chartered Accountants in Scotland	*CA*
The Chartered Insurance Institute	*CII Journal*
The Chartered Institute of Management Accountants	*Management Accounting*
The Institute of Management	*Management Today and Professional Manager*

The daily press provides plenty of material to support the investigative student. Look out for news items, special articles and supplements, and relevant advertising.

Common abbreviations and acronyms

ABF&D	Association of British Factors and Discounters
ABI	Association of British Insurers
ACT	Advance Corporation Tax
AGM	Annual General Meeting
AIM	Alternative Investment Market
APR	Annual Percentage Rate
BACS	Bankers Automated Clearing Services
BIIBA	British Insurance and Investment Brokers' Association
BIS	Banking Information Service
CA	Institute of Chartered Accountants
CBI	Confederation of British Industry
CGT	Capital Gains Tax
CHAPS	Clearing House Automated Payment System
CII	Chartered Insurance Institute
DSS	Department of Social Security
DTI	Department of Trade and Industry
ECGD	Export Credits Guarantee Department
EDI	Electronic Data Interchange
ERM	Exchange Rate Mechanism
FIMBRA	Financial Intermediaries, Managers and Brokers Regulatory Association
FT	*Financial Times*
GAD	Government Actuary's Department
GNVQ	General National Vocational Qualification
HMSO	Her Majesty's Stationery Office
IFA	Independent Financial Adviser
IMRO	Investment Management Regulatory Organisation
IR	Inland Revenue
LAUTRO	Life Assurance and Unit Trust Regulatory Organisation

LCH	London Clearing House
LIBOR	London Inter-Bank Offered Rate
LIFFE	London International Financial Futures and Options Exchange
LINC	Local Investment Networking Company
PYBT	Prince's Youth Business Trust
SEATS	Stock Exchange Alternative Trading Service
SERPS	State Earnings Related Pension Scheme
SIB	Securities and Investments Board
SSAP	Statements of Standard Accounting Practice
SWIFT	Society for Worldwide Interbank Financial Telecommunication
VAT	Value Added Tax

Index